The Idle Investor

Every owner of a physical copy of

The Idle Investor

can download the eBook for free direct from us
at Harriman House, in a format that can be read
on any eReader, tablet or smartphone.

Simply go to:

ebooks.harriman-house.com/idleinvestor

to get your copy now.

The Idle Investor

How to Invest 5 Minutes a Week and Beat the Professionals

Edmund Shing

HARRIMAN HOUSE LTD
18 College Street
Petersfield
Hampshire
GU31 4AD
GREAT BRITAIN
Tel: +44 (0)1730 233870
Email: contact@harriman-house.com
Website: www.harriman-house.com

Paperback ISBN: 9780857193810
eBook ISBN: 9780857194817

British Library Cataloguing in Publication Data

A CIP catalogue record for this book can be obtained from the British Library.

All Figures created by Edmund Shing, with use of external data where attributed.

About the author

Edmund Shing is a Global Equity portfolio manager at BCS Asset Management, focusing on a combination of high-level investment themes and fundamental stock-picking. He is also a consultant for the Opportunité Idle Investor Fund, a French unit trust (SICAV) investing in a variety of smart beta ETFs based on the principles outlined in this book.

Edmund has previously worked at Barclays Capital (as Head of European Equity Strategy), BNP Paribas (as a Prop Trader), Julius Baer, Schroders and Goldman Sachs during a 20-year career in financial markets based in Paris and London. He also holds a PhD in Artificial Intelligence from the University of Birmingham. You can follow him on Twitter @TheIdleInvestor and his website – featuring regular market commentary and investing thoughts – can be found at www.idleinvestor.com.

Acknowledgements

First and most importantly, I would like to thank my wife Kim for all her love, support and patience throughout firstly my doctorate, then my career in finance and most recently the writing of this book. I dedicate this book to her.

My mother and father, Teresa and Yuk Wah, have also been instrumental in my orientation towards education and then finance, having seen the enormous amount of hard work that they have put into their own various businesses over the years. Frankly, after working with them in catering and the hotel trade throughout my student years, one thing I realised very early on was that I wanted a career that was not going to be as tough as catering!

My four children Benjamin, Lucy, Oliver and William have been a key source of inspiration – I originally wrote the book as a form of legacy for them, hoping to give them a simple investing system which they can understand, and that they will be able to follow themselves in the years to come when they start out on their own career paths. So I hope they find the time to read this book and then put the strategies contained within into profitable action.

I want to show gratitude to both my mother- and father-in-law Huw and Heather for reading the manuscript at various stages of development and giving me valuable feedback, preventing me from descending into the language of financial jargon.

Thanks go also to the team at the Paris-based Opportunité société de gestion with whom I work on the Idle Investor fund, a UCITS IV fund based on the principles and strategies outlined in this book, and in particular to Pierre Krief at Opportunité, who has been instrumental in bringing the fund from initial concept to final existence.

Last but not least, my editor Stephen Eckett at Harriman House has been indispensable with his words of advice gleaned from years both writing and publishing financial tomes; I thank Stephen for honing what was initially a rather unwieldy first draft into something that I hope you will find far more readable!

Preface

Who this book is for

Tick all that apply:

- Are you tired of the paltry interest rates on offer at banks and building societies?

- Do you have long-term savings that you probably do not require access to for at least the next three years?

- Are you interested in investment (i.e. growing your own money), and would like to know more?

- Are you unsure where to start when investing your own money?

- Are you cash-rich, but time-poor due to a busy lifestyle?

- Are you concerned about investing in shares given the two sharp drops since 2000?

- Would you like to use a simple investing system that beats the broad markets over time, while limiting the risk taken?

- Would you like to learn an investing system that only needs a few minutes each month?

If you have ticked several of the boxes above, then this is the book for you!

What this book contains

In this book you will find three simple investing systems for long-term savings. Each of these systems require only a limited amount of your time per month and all use low-cost index funds. The simple systems here are mechanical, so there is no need for you to figure out what to do each month – you simply have to consistently follow the system.

The systems are based on five tried and tested, durable share market anomalies that have persisted for a long time.

Of course, as with any investing system, there may be short-term periods of underperformance but the systems outperform in the long-term *as long as you stick to them*. This will therefore require a good amount of self-discipline and patience, but should over time handsomely reward the disciplined, patient investor.

What knowledge is assumed

I've assumed that you are likely to:

1. be interested in investing your own long-term savings in something other than a (very low-yielding) cash deposit account, and

2. have already had some experience in investing, be it via funds of one sort or another (unit trusts, ETFs, investment trusts, pension funds, life assurance products), or even directly in individual shares, bonds and other financial instruments.

If you are a complete novice in the world of investment and have never before bought shares, unit trusts or even funds via an ISA, let me be honest: this is not the ideal first investment book for you. In the Appendix I have listed a number of books that I consider to be excellent introductions to the world of investment. Such an introduction is outside the scope of this book.

In contrast, if you have at least dabbled in investment in shares and bonds, either directly or via funds, then this book could be very useful to you in providing a clear framework for investing in shares and bonds via low-cost funds.

I would also suggest that the investing systems in this book are best applied by those with at least £10,000 of starting capital.

Structure of the book

This book is divided into three main parts:

1. **Part A: Checklist of key investing concepts**. A brief introduction to the investing concepts you should know before investing your own money. This includes various potential homes for your cash savings, and why just taking the easy option of handing control of your investment capital over to active fund managers is not necessarily a good idea.

2. **Part B: Investment building blocks – asset classes, risk and return**. This part does a number of things: (a) it focuses on the relationship between investment risk and reward, (b) it highlights a number of share market anomalies that investors can take advantage of to outperform the broad market, and (c) it also takes an in-depth look at what risks and returns have been generated by major asset classes like shares, government bonds and cash over the last century or so.

3. **Part C: 3 DIY investing systems**. This final part is the DIY section, where I suggest three simple investing systems that all use low-cost and liquid exchange-traded funds as the basic investing vehicle, and which range from yearly rebalancing to monthly reallocation, depending on how lazy you are feeling.

Each of the 12 chapters in this book are relatively self-contained – you can skip straight to one and read it on its own if you wish.

In the Appendix I have included a lot of detail about where to find financial information and ideas on the internet, plus some recommended books on investing for further reading.

Contents

PART A.

Basic Principles

CHAPTER 1.

The Long Path To These Investing Systems

The journey that I have taken to arrive at these three investing systems has been relatively long and involved. I have worked in the financial markets, both in London and Paris, for 20 years, in a number of different roles. This came after I had gained a doctorate in Artificial Intelligence (a subject which, while fascinating to me at the time, had precious little to do with finance of any sort).

I wanted to pursue a career in financial research, but applied research rather than the academic research that I had been engaged in for over three years leading up to that point. So I applied to a large number of research departments, primarily at investment banks based in the venerable City of London.

My first steps in the City

I was finally offered a role to kick-start my post-academic finance career in late 1994 at the pre-eminent US bulge bracket investment bank Goldman Sachs, located in Fleet Street next to the old home of the *Daily Express* newspaper. I started out on day one knowing virtually nothing at all about finance, and was immediately assigned to the equity strategy team, which involved trying to predict the direction of share markets (including trying to forecast year-end levels for indices such as the FTSE 100), and coming up with interesting investment themes that professional investment managers, key clients of the bank, could reflect in their own share portfolios of UK and European companies.

This was a great experience for a newbie to the world of finance, as it involved a lot of on-the-job training and learning fast, usually doing long hours as a junior investment analyst. However, I quickly became quite cynical about the claims of so-called City experts to be able to predict or forecast the direction of the economy or financial markets (e.g. share or foreign exchange markets) given the complexity of the problem. Frankly, it is just too difficult, particularly when you consider the potential impact of exogenous events like the Gulf War or the bankruptcy of Lehman Brothers.

The first key lesson that I took away from my full-time job in the City

Don't waste your time trying to forecast future levels of share market indices like the FTSE 100! There are so many macro-economic, geopolitical and share-specific factors at work that you have little chance of being right on a consistent basis.

A very British change of culture

Upon leaving Goldman Sachs together with my then-boss after a couple of years, I embarked on a similar equity strategy role at another City institution, but this time a British investment bank – Schroders. This was a very different culture, where the atmosphere was perhaps less aggressive than it had been at times at Goldmans, and where the emphasis was much more on producing a high standard of research on share market investment themes than on writing and marketing weekly research.

This second stint in the City taught me the value of standing back from the daily hurly-burly of share market trading, to try to distance myself from the inevitable volatility of rising and falling markets and shares, and instead to try to focus on a select few key trending investment themes at any given moment. I also learnt that if these investment themes were identified relatively early on, then they could remain valid for a number of months or even years, and result in sizeable trends in individual shares, industry sectors or even entire financial markets over that period.

Lesson 2

Long-term investment trends can last a surprisingly long time, far longer than we might expect and even sometimes spanning several years. In addition, they can be very profitable for those who (a) manage to identify the trend early on, and (b) have the confidence and resolve to stick with that trend until it is finally exhausted.

Moving to Gay Paree

Unfortunately, one day in early 2000, I discovered along with my Schroder colleagues that our section of the Schroders business, the investment bank (as distinct from the fund management division that still today bears the Schroders name) was to be sold to the US bank Citigroup, to be merged into their investment banking and broking division Salomon Smith Barney (SSB). This would entail working with new colleagues from SSB in Canary Wharf to the east of London, rather than right by St. Paul's Cathedral in the heart of the City, where the Schroders building stood.

Not enamoured by the prospect of working for a second US investment bank, nor with relocating to Canary Wharf, I instead opted to take the role of Head of the European Equity Strategy team at the investment broking division of the Swiss private bank, Julius Baer, based in Paris. I spent seven years working for this firm in equity research (writing and marketing research reports about key investment themes pertaining to the European share markets), also working for a time in research sales.

This latter role involved taking the research reports that I and other research analysts produced on various investment ideas on share markets and individual companies, and marketing them via telephone, email or even face-to-face meetings to large investment fund managers in the City and throughout the wider world.

At this point I really started to appreciate the various layers of cost that were being laid on the average retail fund client (who owns units in a unit trust or private pension). Not only did:

- the fund manager have to be paid (normally a rather large salary), and also

- the back office staff of the fund manager who take care of all the trading and subsequent administration, and then finally

- the various share brokers providing investment ideas to the various fund managers who would then have to pay their own research analysts, salespeople and traders out of the commission paid by the fund managers for shares bought and sold on their behalf.

All in all this seemed to be a rather convoluted and expensive way for fund managers to try to beat the performance of the reference share market index (e.g. the FTSE 100 in the UK, or the Euro STOXX in continental Europe). And, more often than not, they would fail to achieve this key objective of beating the market in a consistent manner.

Lesson 3

The majority of active fund managers do not manage to earn their fund clients a consistently better investment return than the share market averages over time, and moreover charge their clients handsomely for this failure, as they also have to compensate share brokers for their research efforts.

After all this time I thought I could do better at share market investment than many of my fund manager clients, and looked for an opportunity to try my hand at investing ('walking the walk' rather than simply 'talking the talk', as I had done for nearly 12 years up to that point).

My investment efforts with my own savings had been generally profitable but very volatile up to then, with several very painful episodes where I had managed to make big dents in my investment capital through big losses on investments, notably during the 2000-2003 global bear market when share market indexes lost around 50% of their value.

The pressure cooker environment of proprietary trading

In 2007 I managed to land a job as a proprietary trader at the French bank BNP Paribas, based in the centre of Paris a stone's throw from the *Grands Magasins* on Boulevard Haussmann. I was to run a proprietary book for BNP, effectively using the bank's own money to make more money by investing in a number of different asset classes (i.e. shares, bonds, currency, commodities) using a global macro strategy which tried to identify big investment trends and then profit from them; investing either long (expecting the assets to go up in value) or short (selling these assets, then expecting their prices to fall before then buying them back cheaper and pocketing the difference).

This all sounds very exciting, doesn't it? But the reality was quite different – hours on end spent staring at computer screens, agonising over whether to put a trade on or not, and then agonising once again over whether to cut a trade and take a loss, or to take profits before a given target had been reached.

This type of trading meant frequently not being able to go out of the office even for a short period of time while the markets were open, particularly at the open (the first 30 minutes of the European trading day from 8am UK time), the US open (typically at 2:30pm UK time each weekday), and then at the market close (the last 30 minutes before share markets closed for the day, typically 4:30pm UK time) when there was often a lot of movement in the various share and bond markets.

Lesson 4

Obsessive screen-watching tends to be deleterious for your long-term financial and mental health, as you are tempted to panic into and out of investments. Full-time trading of this nature requires a remarkably cool temperament (as devoid of emotion as possible), and also requires the development of, and strict adherence to, an investment system to have any chance of long-term success.

As a result of this trading experience at BNP Paribas, towards the end of which I experienced the extreme market volatility caused in late 2008 by the failure of the US investment bank Lehman Brothers, I now have little faith in any form of short-term day-trading strategy.

In contrast, I have developed a deep-seated appreciation for the use of a battery of financial market indicators to give a better sense of underlying trends in markets, to complement any form of fundamental analysis (based for instance on macroeconomic data or investment themes).

Lesson 5

Your best chance of investment success in the long term lies in keeping costs to a minimum via resisting the urge to trade too often (i.e. over-trading), and in following a clearly-defined investment methodology or system involving the use of specific financial market indicators as a guide. Risk management (e.g. knowing when to cut your losses on a given investment position) is an under-appreciated but vital element in any successful investing system.

It was also at BNP Paribas that I spent a year working in derivatives research (working in futures and options, but also index-related products like exchange-traded funds (ETFs) and structured products). I started to work more and more on multi-asset research, tying together the best ideas of research analysts in bonds, commodities and foreign exchange, combined with our own work on share markets, to come up with investment themes that spanned these various asset classes, and also working on how best to allocate investment capital between these various asset classes, the process called *asset allocation*.

This process is especially important for large long-term investment funds like pension funds or life insurance funds, where there is a need to generate a relatively consistent rate of return and also spread risk rather than concentrating it in just one asset class like government bonds or shares.

Lesson 6

Asset allocation is a very important way to reduce your investment risk over time via diversification. However, most investors have relatively unsophisticated ways of deciding the asset allocation for their funds, and often use basic (and arbitrary) benchmarks as their guide.

Back to Blighty

My last few years have been spent employed back in the UK, firstly in research at Barclays Capital (BarCap for short), the investment banking arm of the UK retail bank Barclays. At BarCap, I spent an increasing amount of my time working on multi-asset investment themes and asset allocation, and spent quite some time reading the academic research surrounding asset allocation.

I became increasingly convinced that while asset allocation was in principle a necessary investment process for any long-term investor, that investor would be best served by a straightforward multi-asset investing system using simple-to-understand signals to direct the allocation of capital to the various asset classes.

I also spent an increasing amount of time reading up on the academic research surrounding the concept of trending; that is to say that once any financial market establishes a trend (either up or down), the trend tends to persist for a relatively long period of time, usually far longer than one would expect. This goes against the classical financial theory of efficient markets, which states basically that financial markets move in a random-walk fashion. However, we can observe that financial markets *can* trend for a long time, i.e. that we have a good chance of predicting where a given financial market is going next simply by looking at where the market has just come from.

Lesson 7

In the long-term, momentum and trend-following have been surprisingly successful ways to invest in various financial markets. However, they are subject to wide swings in performance, suggesting that a robust method for controlling financial risk is also needed when following trends.

Focusing on the index world

Following BarCap, there then followed a short stint as investment strategist at the financial index provider S&P Dow Jones Indices, which allowed me the opportunity to extensively research the concept of smart beta indices. These are indices that aim to outperform the classical benchmark share market indices like the FTSE 100 or S&P 500, both of which are market-capitalisation weighted – which means that the larger the overall market value of a company's shares, the greater the weighting that company has in the index.

In the case of the FTSE 100, this means that the likes of oil companies BP and Shell, telecom company Vodafone and healthcare companies GlaxoSmithKline and AstraZeneca dominate the index, leading to a heavy level of concentration of the Footsie in just a few companies. This is the opposite of diversification and can lead to a high level of financial risk being present in a benchmark index like the FTSE 100, as we found out in recent years when BP was hit by the Macondo oil disaster in the Gulf of Texas, sending its share price plummeting and the value of the FTSE 100 with it.

Smart beta indices work in a number of different ways both to select the members of an index and then to decide the weighting that each member should have in the final index, rather than simply choosing the largest companies by market value and then weighting them accordingly in the benchmark index. The simplest form of smart beta index is an equal-weight index, where each member has exactly the same importance or weight in the index. In the case of the FTSE 100, that would mean that each member of the index would have a weighting of 1% of the index, as there are 100 members in total.

Equal-weight share market indices have been shown to outperform their market-value weighted counterparts over long periods of time. And yet investing today remains focused on the market value-weighted benchmark indices, despite their obvious weaknesses.

Most importantly, the universe of low-cost ETFs that track a wide variety of smart beta indices has expanded rapidly in recent years. This allows the retail investor access to a wide range of different, effective investing strategies without the need to pay an expensive fund manager.

Lesson 8

There is now a dizzying array of smart beta index-based ETFs available to the retail investor that allow access to these investment strategies at low cost. The universe of ETFs is expanding all the time, presenting a real challenge to existing actively-managed funds.

Putting the eight lessons into practice

My research over the years has acted as the bedrock for the various multi-asset investing systems that you see presented here. I have taken these eight lessons that I have gleaned over my career in financial markets as my starting point, looking to develop simple investing systems that can help people to invest their long-term savings:

1. without the need to pay an expensive fund manager,

2. spreading investment risk across a number of asset classes,

3. using a momentum-based system at its core to follow market trends, and

4. taking advantage of low-cost, smart beta-based ETFs in order to outperform the benchmark financial market indices in the long-term.

What is more, each of these strategies are not only simple to operate but also take very little time. Even in the most intensive case, you will only need to spend an hour or two per month – perfect for an Idle Investor!

CHAPTER 2.

How Is It Possible To Be An Idle Investor? Quite Easily...

Introducing the Seven Idle Investor Axioms

Does investing have to be complicated? Not at all!

Investment is a topic that can often seem impenetrable to the outsider. There is a lot of jargon that flies around in discussion of investments and financial markets, so it is perhaps no surprise if the lay observer gets the impression that you need to be a real expert in the field to have any chance of success.

In fact, if there is one observation that I feel I can make after my 20 years of working in financial markets, it is that nothing can be further from the truth! To be frank, I have worked with many colleagues who may be experts in their own very narrow field within finance and yet are absolutely hopeless when it comes to their own investments.

There is in French a fine idiom to describe this: *les cordonniers sont toujours les plus mal chaussés*, which translates as 'the cobblers always have the worst shoes'. This is a very apt expression to describe those working in financial markets and their personal portfolio of investments. Typically, colleagues I have worked with in various investment banks take too much risk in their own investments and typically do not even invest according to a particular game plan. In short, experience in and knowledge of financial markets are no guarantee of success in investment!

Let's face it, in the financial world there is a great tendency to make the topic sound more complicated than it is in reality, so as to make the speaker sound more authoritative and knowledgeable. Of course, this is not just true in finance; it is true in many other walks of life, such as computing, law and management, which all have their own lexicon of specialised jargon that can sound like complete gobbledegook to the uninitiated outsider.

However, despite George Bernard Shaw's quip that "All professions are conspiracies against the laity," this is not necessarily a conspiracy. It is just that it is pretty difficult to explain a complicated concept in simple terms and most people have no idea how to do it! One of the missions I have in this book is to explain each investment concept simply, in terms that anyone – for instance those in my own family – can understand, without the need for a diploma in finance.

You can be an idle investor

Not only can investing be much simpler than most investment professionals would have you believe, but it does not have to take up an awful lot of your time. If you follow the right investing system (and stick with it), a lot of the worry and effort can be taken out of investing, with superior results.

The first step on this path to investing simplicity are the Seven Idle Investor Axioms, that I have formulated to capture the essence of the three investing systems I will lay out later in this book. These seven axioms are here to help you be an idle, but profitable, investor over the long haul. I will be returning to these axioms time and time again.

The starting point: the Seven Idle Investor Axioms

These seven key guidelines are designed to point you towards succeeding over the long term with your own investment portfolio, using a simple, rule-based investing method that only requires a little of your time once per month.

Axiom 1. Keep investing simple

This rule is applicable to life generally, not only to investing. First of all, any successful investor that I have ever met or even just read about has at heart a simple method that drives how they invest. Investing is all about getting from your starting point (your current savings and future spare cash to save) to your investment end-point, be that a very long-term goal like a comfortable retirement, or a shorter-term goal such as building up a nest egg for your children. The terrain you must navigate can be full of unknown twists and turns, as the financial markets are rarely calm waters to navigate.

So you would be better to be armed for this investing journey with an investing roadmap to guide you and keep you on track to reach your goals. The simpler this roadmap is, the easier it will be to follow, even in the face of unexpected events or obstacles, such as natural or man-made catastrophes. Having a simple rulebook to follow under these circumstances makes it easier for any investor to keep a clear head and not panic.

I have in the past worked in equity derivatives research, writing reports about often arcane and complicated investment strategies using futures and options. While often a fascinating subject, it has a tendency to become overly mathematical in nature, making you feel that you need a doctorate in applied maths just to understand how the particular options strategy is meant to work. In reality, many of these derivatives strategies serve to enrich the investment bank selling the strategy, rather than the end clients. This is a particular criticism that I have of the structured products arena, where these complicated derivatives-based investment strategies become financial products that are then sold to retail clients, who have no hope of understanding the mechanics behind the strategy.

As a result I have never bought a structured product for myself, as I know how complicated the underlying investment strategy is, and how much money the bank is likely to make out of it irrespective of whether I actually make any money myself. Better instead to keep your investment goals and strategies simple, to improve your chances of long-term success.

Axiom 2. Don't invest in what you do not understand

This desire for simplicity in investing then leads me on to the second Idle Investor Axiom: Do not invest in what you do not understand.

A marketing pitch for a given investment product may sound very seductive, offering the opportunity to make untold investment gains on your initial invested capital. But don't be drawn in like a fly to a spider's web; if you don't understand clearly how these investment gains can be made, don't fall for the marketing pitch.

This is a variant on the old adage: if it sounds too good to be true, then it probably is. In the end, those that invested in Bernie Madoff's hedge fund on the basis of the fantastic returns he offered, but without understanding how he generated these amazing investment returns, all fell prey to this trap. And as it turned out in the case of the infamous Madoff, he could not in reality produce these investment returns, but instead was running a pyramid scheme (using inflows from new investors to pay the investment returns he promised to old investors).

Even as eminent and experienced an investor as Warren Buffett (one of the richest men in the world, as if you didn't already know!), invests according to this maxim. He completely missed out on the US technology boom of the late 1990s, as he admitted later that he simply couldn't understand what these companies did or what their business model was. For a couple of years the performance of his investment vehicle Berkshire Hathaway suffered in comparison to the US share market, as these technology shares racked up huge price gains. But then in the bust that followed he massively outperformed the US share market as it was dragged down by a collapse in the share prices of the very same technology companies.

This is one of the reasons why I do not invest in certain sectors, such as biotechnology companies (but only after burning my fingers on a couple of not-so-successful shares). I feel that I have no way to judge the potential success or failure of pharmaceutical drugs under development. Through painful personal experience, I have learned only to invest in companies and investment strategies that I can understand.

Axiom 3. Don't follow financial markets on a daily basis

This advice may sound a little rich, coming from someone who has spent years of his life in front of computer screens with company share prices and index levels constantly moving up and down in a dizzying array of colours and signals. But remember, I do this because I work in the financial markets. As an investment strategist at a number of banks in the past, I have had to be prepared to get up and speak at a moment's notice on the back of a particularly noteworthy item of news, such as the latest economic data releases and their potential impact on the share markets.

From the point of view of pure investment, an investor can make his or her own life much easier, and be a true Idle Investor, by simply ignoring pretty much all of this news flow. For a start, the vast majority of so-called business news is simply noise and chatter that does not have any significant bearing on the long-term direction of shares or financial markets. Secondly, most people reading this book will have full-time jobs to attend to in order to pay the bills (and hopefully have some money left over to invest at the end of the day). In which case, they simply do not have the time to follow the financial markets in real time, as they have their own daily lives to lead.

The good news is that you simply do not need to follow financial markets on a live, or even daily, basis in order to follow a successful investment strategy for your own savings. In fact, I believe it is definitely detrimental to your personal investment performance, as constant monitoring of markets and associated news flow can serve to make any investor anxious and nervous, and thus prone to making the wrong short-term investment decisions.

Again, this is a lesson that I have had to learn through painful personal experience. I cannot recall the number of times that I have followed every item of news flow on a particular share that I have bought after lengthy analysis and research, only then to sell it prematurely on the back of one piece of news that I judged to be negative for the company. And then subsequently to see the company's share price surge higher on the back of the strong fundamental story that I had correctly identified in the first place! So on many occasions I have ended up making just a small gain on a share that has gone on to double or more. I won't name the shares in this case, because it is just too painful to recall just how much I have missed out on, all because I allowed the daily news flow to get the better of me and cause me to panic sell.

So, yes, it is great to take an interest in financial markets and to read the business section of a daily or weekly newspaper (I particularly recommend the *Economist* and the weekend edition of the *Financial Times*, and the *Financial Mail* is also not at all bad). But don't be tempted to screen-watch during the day – find something else more enriching to do with your time.

Axiom 4. Harness the incredible power of compound interest

Albert Einstein said, "The most powerful force in the universe is compound interest." Put simply, the longer you leave your savings to compound up using a particular investment strategy, the more they will grow at an increasingly faster rate over time. It is quite astounding how much difference even 1% more in annual investment gains makes over a number of years. This is linked to the previous axiom, as it does involve not being tempted by short-term gyrations in share prices (either up or down) to sell out of a given investment.

You would do well to remember that the two most common mistakes that people make with their investments are (a) selling too soon when they have started to make some gains, forgoing future gains, and (b) selling out in a panic when the share market takes a tumble, as does happen from time to time. In either case you are not allowing the law of compound interest to work its magic on your investment capital.

Let's compare two situations where we invest in the FTSE 100.

- **Case 1**: we invest £100 in the FTSE 100 in 1994 and keep any dividends received over the subsequent 20 years in cash (the column marked 'Not Compounded' in Figure 1).

- **Case 2**: we systematically reinvest all dividends received over time back into the FTSE 100 index and don't draw out any dividends as cash at all (the column marked 'Compounded' in Figure 1).

Figure 1: £100 invested in the FTSE 100 index: 1994-2014

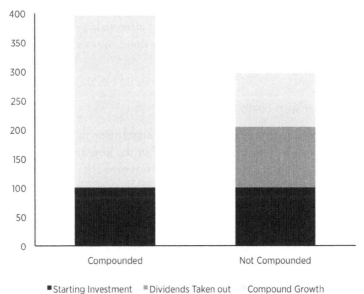

Source: FTSE.

Now, let's look at the respective results after 20 years.

- **Case 1** (dividends received kept in cash) saw the initial £100 investment grow into just over £200 over the 1994-2014 period. To that we add the accumulated dividends received in cash of over £90, giving us £191 of gains over the 20 years (i.e. nearly tripling our original investment). Not bad.

- **Case 2** (dividends reinvested in the FTSE 100 index each time) saw the initial £100 grow to just under £400, including all dividends reinvested. Now that is a near-quadrupling of the original £100; an improvement of 50% over the performance of Case 1.

This is the power of the compound interest effect: if you continually reinvest all income received from your investment, over time you earn more income on that income, which can make a very big difference to your overall investment returns in the long term.

This all serves to illustrate that if you pick a good investment, and are not tempted to sell in the short-term after making some gains, it can go on to multiply those gains many times over the years, thanks to the beauty of compound interest.

Axiom 5. Keep costs low

Every small increment in your annual investment return can make a big difference to your invested capital in the long run. One of the key ways to improve your net investment return is to keep the costs of investing low.

That means, if you are buying individual shares, keeping the transaction costs low by choosing a good discount broker. In the case of unit trusts, investment trusts and exchange-traded funds, this means choosing funds with low annual management charges and preferably no initial or exit charges to boot. That way, you maximise your net annual investment return and allow your capital to grow, without unnecessarily enriching the fund manager along the way.

In my case, I like to use exchange-traded funds for the most part when investing using funds, as they have no entry or exit charges, and typically have low annual management fees as well – usually far lower than you would find on equivalent unit trusts. ETFs are also good in that they typically have lower annual management fees than equivalent unit trusts (although you do have to pay 0.5% stamp duty when you buy an ETF, as with any UK-quoted share). With ETFs, there will also be a dealing charge starting at around £7.50 per trade with the cheapest brokers for each ETF you buy and sell. For a portfolio size of £10,000 these dealing charges are negligible and I estimate them to be around 0.3% per deal.

If you are going to pay the extra cost for a particular fund manager, try to ensure that you are truly paying for superior long-term performance. You can skew the odds in your favour by using active fund managers only in a select number of investment areas where they have proven as a group to have outperformed the relevant benchmark indices over the long-term in the past, for example:

1. small-caps (UK, US or Europe),

2. Japanese shares, and

3. high-yield corporate bonds.

If instead you are going to invest in large-cap shares, then it is difficult to see how fund managers can outperform the benchmark indices by enough to justify their higher fees.

Axiom 6. Keep the faith, even when financial markets take a tumble

This can be summed up as: don't panic!

Of course, there are times when it is better to retreat to safer investments, like government bonds or even cash during the recession from the middle of 2007 to the end of 2008. But looking back at the history of financial markets since the beginning of the 20th century, these occasions are relatively few and far between.

So, in general, even if the share markets drop by 10% or so (what is called a *market correction* in financial jargon), it is usually better to remain invested over the period, rather than try to time the markets by selling during the downturn, and then attempting to time your re-entry. Chances are that when the share market hits a bottom, you will be too scared of further falls to buy back in.

This is one of the typical traps that we humans fall into when investing, being ruled by our emotions rather than by rational logic. Think about it: if we go shopping and see the price of a new flat-screen television reduced by 20% in a sale, we would normally be keener to buy it as it looks to be a bargain. However, when we see the same 20% reduction in prices during a share market downturn, we are generally unwilling to buy the market at 20% off its previous level, as we are so scared that it will fall further.

Incidentally, the potential for the TV's price to be reduced further does not generally stop people buying the TV, so as long-term investors why should we think that way about financial investments? This is exactly what the field of behavioural finance examines – the times when we seem unable to follow rational logic, instead driven by our own emotions to make what turn out to be poor investing decisions.

If you really want to follow an investment strategy that times the markets and sells when there is a significant downturn, then you can simply follow the third of the three Idle Investor strategies outlined later, rather than try to time the markets yourself and be influenced by your own emotions.

Axiom 7. Keep a buffer fund in cash for unforeseen emergencies and opportunities

And to the seventh and final Idle Investor axiom, keeping a buffer fund in cash. Why would you bother, I hear you ask, particularly in this day and age when interest rates on savings accounts are so low?

Well, there are two good reasons for keeping a cash buffer. The first is simply to prepare for any unexpected spending that may happen in life, such as repairing a roof or a car. You don't want to have to cash in your investments, potentially at a bad time, just because you have some large expense that suddenly arises.

The second reason is more investment-related: it is so that you can take advantage of any temporary investing opportunity, for instance if the share market sells off sharply. If you have cash reserves ready to hand, you can then invest when an outstanding opportunity presents itself, without necessarily having to sell other investments at a time which may be less than optimal.

Typically, even in a bull market where shares are in a rising trend, there are at least a couple of occasions when share markets correct, or sell off by at least 10% in short order, driven by some fear or other. If you have cash reserves ready to hand at that point, you can potentially supercharge your investment portfolio returns by putting the cash to work in the financial markets at that moment.

Recap: the Seven Idle Investor Axioms

Let's quickly recap the Seven Idle Investor Axioms, as we will be returning to them when we discuss the three Idle Investor strategies for managing an investment portfolio.

1. Keep investing simple.

2. Don't invest in what you do not understand.

3. Don't follow financial markets on a daily basis.

4. Harness the incredible power of compound interest over time.

5. Keep costs low to maximise the compound interest effect.

6. Keep the faith, even when financial markets take a tumble.

7. Keep a buffer fund in cash for unforeseen emergencies and opportunities.

Now you have the Seven Idle Investor Axioms, what next?

CHAPTER 3.

Why You Should Not Give Your Money To A Fund Manager

DIY Investing is the way to go!

We are now going to put the Seven Idle Investor Axioms into practice.

After reading the previous chapter, you might think that the easiest way to follow Axiom 1 (*keep things simple*) is to buy an actively-managed investment fund like a unit trust, and let the fund manager do the hard work of investing your money for you.

This sounds a seductively simple solution, right? Unfortunately, matters are rarely this simple – there is a high price to pay for following this hands-off strategy to managing your investment portfolio. And on top of that, it doesn't solve all your problems, as you still need to pick a fund or a number of funds to invest in.

How do you choose an actively-managed unit trust?

So to start with: how do you even decide which fund or funds to put your money into? On the Investment Association website (theinvestmentassociation.org), there are as many as 2,345 separate unit trusts listed, with many classifications for these funds, including:

1. by fund focus (income, growth, balanced investment),

2. by asset type (shares, property, government bonds, corporate bonds, cash-like instruments),

3. by geographic exposure (UK, continental Europe, US, Japan, emerging markets), and

4. by ways to invest (in a single lump sum, with monthly contributions, through tax-advantaged accounts like an ISA).

Then there is the question of how you choose which unit trust management company or companies to use, given that there are over 200 in the UK alone. Put simply, even if you were to go down this route of handing over your savings to an external active fund manager, there is still a pretty complex set of decisions to be made before arriving at a choice of fund or funds to invest in. Not so simple after all, eh?

Remember Axiom 5: keep costs low

In returning to Axiom 5 on keeping investing costs as low as possible, I want to convince you that DIY investing is the way to go, and that relying on active fund managers to invest your savings for you typically results in subpar growth for your savings, net of all costs.

Remember that the benefit of keeping investment costs low is the maximising of the effect of growth on your investment portfolio. Well, I am going to demonstrate that the higher charges that you pay in using an actively-managed investment fund, like a unit trust, result in a lower rate of growth for your savings over the long term.

But first, a confession...

Before I go any further, I feel I should come clean. My day job is as a fund manager! So here I am, suggesting that giving your savings to an active fund manager to invest is not the way to achieve the best long-term investment growth. But that is precisely the job I do on a day-to-day basis – isn't that rather contradictory?

Okay, yes it is true that I am currently employed as a fund manager for foreign clients. But let me make a few points in my defence:

1. Much of what I do is built on the back of data-based screening techniques for finding ETFs and individual shares that are based on well-established value and momentum-based effects outlined in academic research for outperforming the wider share markets. I will go into some detail on what these various market-beating effects are, and how I use them in selecting ETFs for my three investing systems, in a later chapter.

2. I also make much use of smart beta ETFs in a simple yet effective fashion to outperform the benchmark share market indices, while keeping management costs low and still benefiting from well-diversified portfolios.

3. I make a great effort to keep buying and selling of ETFs and shares in my funds to a minimum, in order to keep overall trading costs as low as possible.

So while I work as a fund manager for my day job, I hope I have managed to convince you that this is not, after all, at odds with the seven investing axioms that I described earlier.

And now, a look at the disadvantages of using active fund managers.

The disadvantages of using active fund managers

One of the reasons that you would consider buying a unit trust run by an active fund manager rather than a passive index-tracking fund like an ETF is that the fund manager is an expert in matters of long-term investment in his or her chosen area, such as in UK shares or in US government bonds.

They should know better than you and better than a passive index like the FTSE 100 which are the best shares or bonds to buy for the best long-term investment returns, and this superior knowledge should allow them to select investments that outperform the broad market indices, which is what passive index funds mimic.

So with passive funds you should receive the performance of the underlying share or bond market (less management costs), while active funds should benefit from the experience and skill of fund managers to outperform these market indices.

How often do active fund managers beat benchmark indices, after fees?

However, think about this for a minute: how do you actually know that they *are* experts in their chosen field of investment? Of course, they will tell you that they are, and the marketing literature published by their fund management company will point to their experience and long-term investment performance. But how can we *know* for sure?

Much of the marketing material on actively-managed unit trusts highlights the historic performance of their fund over a number of years (typically one, three, and five years, and maybe also ten years). This may look very impressive. However, you should not take these numbers necessarily as proof that these funds, even if they have outperformed benchmark indices like the FTSE 100 or the S&P 500 in the past, will continue to do so in the future.

From academic research into this subject, I have discovered some rather surprising conclusions. For instance, according to a 2010 paper, out of 2,076 US domestic mutual funds (what Americans call unit trusts) that existed over the 31 years between 1975 and 2006, 75.4% do *not* beat their benchmark indices after fees are deducted, 24.0% actually do significantly worse than their benchmark indices after fees, and only a measly 0.6% (yes, you read that right, 0.6% – i.e. a lot less than 1%!) of all these US mutual funds actually managed to deliver investment performance net of fees that beat their index benchmarks.[1]

The authors also concluded that even when a fund manager does outperform his or her benchmark index over a number of years, that this is often simply due to them being lucky.

Let's face it; out of more than 2,000 funds, you would expect a significant number of them to do better than the market over a number of years, just due to the sheer number of fund managers who are playing this investment game.

A number of academic studies have determined that it usually takes around 17-25 years to separate true investment skill from simple dumb luck. And the vast majority of the 2,000+ actively-managed unit trusts in the UK do not have anything like such a long track record of outperformance. It is extremely unlikely, even if the fund has existed that long, that the same manager or group of managers has managed the fund for the duration of its life.

The basic take-away is this:

> Most published track records of unit trust performance may look superficially attractive and seductive when presented in a glossy colour brochure, but in fact do not prove anything about the true investment skill of the person or group of people managing the fund, from a statistical point of view.

Most active fund managers underperform benchmark indices over time

To back up this statement, I point you to the statistical work done by Standard & Poor's with their SPIVA (S&P Indices Versus Active Funds). As of the end of 2011, approximately 60% of US equity mutual funds underperformed the broad US equity index over the previous ten years, with as much as 90% of these funds

---

1 Barras, Scaillet and Wermers, 'False Discoveries in Mutual Fund Performance: Measuring Luck in Estimated Alphas' (2010).

underperforming the equity market over the 12 months to mid-2012 (see Figure 2).[2]

Figure 2: The percentage of US mutual funds that underperformed over five years versus S&P index benchmarks

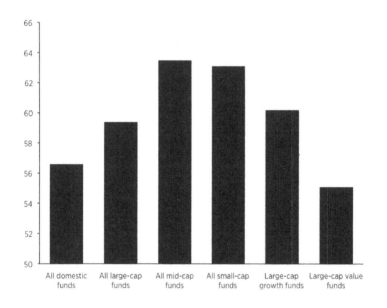

Source: Standard & Poor's.

That is all very well, you might say, but surely UK-based fund managers have done a better job of performing against their respective benchmark indices, adding value by picking better or cheaper companies than the market average? Unfortunately, the official statistics from the industry body, the Investment Association (IA), does not support this assertion at all. I have included the ten-year returns before fees from six broad IA fund categories, the first four for equities and the last two for sovereign bonds, in Figure 3.

---

2 Standard & Poor's, us.spindices.com/resource-center/thought-leadership/spiva

Figure 3: UK fund managers have on average underperformed benchmarks since 2002

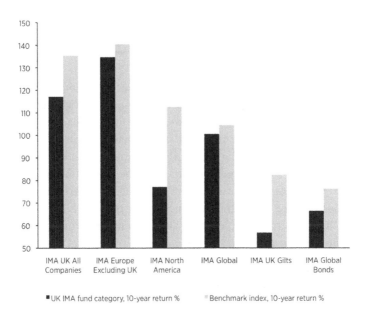

■ UK IMA fund category, 10-year return %   ▨ Benchmark index, 10-year return %

Source: Investment Association; Bloomberg.

Out of these six categories, the average actively managed fund has not managed to beat the index benchmark even once since September 2002. So much for the theory that these active fund managers can add value to investors' savings over and above the market index with their professional skills

Of course, these are just average fund performance statistics, so within these numbers there will be a significant number of managers that have beaten the index averages over the last ten years – but this is clearly not at all true for the profession as a whole.

Observation number 1

The majority of active fund managers underperform equity indices over any extended period of time.

You should also bear in mind that I have not yet accounted for the impact from fees. According to the fund manager SCM Private, the 3,401 active retail funds they surveyed in the UK had an average annual management fee of 1.5% and a total expense ratio (TER) of an even higher 1.63% p.a.[3] This is without taking into account any entry and exit charges that may also be levied on these active funds, which can be as much as 6% on a one-off basis on top of the management fee. In contrast, a typical index-tracking ETF mirroring these indices carries a typical annual management fee of 0.4%-0.5% and no entry or exit fees.

Observation number 2

Fund managers are on average not worth the additional fees they charge over and above an equivalent index-tracking fund.

Beware the undermining effect of high trading costs or fund charges

A very important investment topic concerns the ravaging effect of trading costs on your investment capital over time.

Let's take a very simple example to illustrate this. The UK equity unit trust of a well-known British fund manager which is a big player

---

3 SCM Private: www.fundweb.co.uk/fund-news/news/scm-hits-out-at-ima-over-fund-fees-claim/1057660.article

in unit trusts has a number of charges[4] that can be applied to the unsuspecting investor:

1. an **initial charge** of 3.25%,

2. a **yearly management charge** of 1.50%, and

3. a **bid-offer spread** (i.e. the difference in daily price when buying or selling units in this fund) of 4.5%.

If we apply this battery of charges to the performance of the average fund in the Investment Management Association's UK All Companies category, we can see in Figure 4 that the average investor who put £100 into the average UK All Companies fund at the end of October 2002 would have ended up with £193.80 by the end of October 2012, with all charges and the cost of buying and selling factored in. In contrast, if that same investor had put the same £100 into the Legal & General UK equities index fund, he or she would now be sitting on £210.50, net of all charges.[5]

Just for the sake of completeness, the reference FTSE All-Share equity index delivered a theoretical net total return (price performance plus dividends received and reinvested over the holding period) of 121% over this ten-year period, turning £100 at the start into £221 before any costs are taken into consideration.

In other words, the total cost of buying, holding and then selling this index through a *passive* index fund was £10.50 on the original £100, whereas the total cost of buying, holding and selling the average *actively-managed* unit trust based on the same universe of UK companies over the same ten years was £27.20, which is more than twice the cost.

So not only did the average fund manager in this fund sector *not* outperform the market over the last ten years, but when all typical charges are included, the average fund in fact returned some 16.8% less over the last ten years versus the Legal & General UK equities

---

4 Source for fund charge information: FE Trustnet.

5 I'm using the Legal & General fund as an example of an index fund; the figures for similar funds from other fund managers would be not be very different.

index fund (which carries no initial charge, a yearly management fee of 0.4% and no bid-offer spread on pricing of the units).

The reference FTSE All-Share index delivered an 8.3% compound annual growth rate (CAGR) in net total return terms over the ten years to October 2012, pre-costs. The actual net investment return of the Legal & General UK index fund over the same period was a 7.7% CAGR, after costs. But, the average IMA UK All Companies unit trust delivered only a 6.8% CAGR over the ten years to October 2012 after all typical costs. This is some 0.9% per year worse off on average than the Legal & General index fund. Compounded over the ten years, this 0.9% annual gap turned into a total performance gap of 16.8% (£16.80), which is quite a considerable chunk of the original £100 invested.

Figure 4: Over the last ten years, active managers costs 16.8% more than a UK index fund

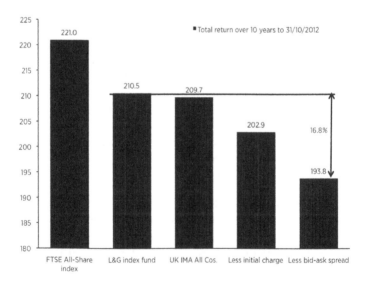

Source: Investment Association; Legal & General; Bloomberg.

Observation 3

Beware the insidious effects of initial and annual charges and other costs on long-term investment performance when choosing funds. Index funds and ETFs are usually a better vehicle than actively-managed funds given their lower cost structure.

Conclusion: active fund management is generally not worth the fees charged

I would argue that the mass of evidence points to active fund management in general not being good value for money, with low-cost index funds and ETFs a better choice for investors, with the exception of a couple of asset classes such as Japanese shares and small-cap share funds, where some active managers have managed to outperform indices substantially over time.

The three Idle Investor strategies that I outline in Part C are all based on the use of index-based ETFs, which allow for low-cost strategies that are also relatively flexible.

PART B.

Investment Building Blocks

CHAPTER 4.

Our Investment Building Blocks: Shares, Bonds And Cash

*Looking at the risk and return of
these three major asset classes*

What are the three Idle Investor strategies going to invest in? Well, the four largest asset classes for the purposes of long-term investment are:

1. **shares** (also called equities in financial literature),

2. **bonds** (both government and corporate; also called fixed income),

3. **cash** (and other cash-like instruments), and

4. **property** (both residential and commercial).

For the purposes of the three Idle Investor strategies, we are going to use the first three – shares, bonds and cash – as they all perform differently under differing economic conditions.

Why I don't use property in my three investment strategies

While we could also use property as an asset class for long-term investment purposes, and many professional investors do indeed invest large sums into property (mostly commercial property such as offices, warehouses and shopping centres), we will not.

Why not?

Well, because I assume that you, as with the majority of the UK adult population, already have heavy exposure to property via owning your own home – so you probably don't need any more. In addition, for the purposes of our three simple investment strategies, property exposure doesn't really offer any additional investment exposure that we do not already capture with a combination of shares, bonds and cash.

Furthermore, buying and selling property is nothing like as easy as buying and selling shares or bonds; it generally takes a long time to complete a property transaction, of the order of weeks or months each time. On top of that, it is a lot more expensive in terms of transaction costs (paying a solicitor, a surveyor, stamp duty, and other incidental costs). So it is not really an asset class that can be easily traded. For these reasons, I am sticking to using the three asset classes of shares, bonds and cash.

Comparing performance of different investments over time: the concept of compound annual growth rate

Let's look at two investments:

1. Investment A increased 45% over seven years.

2. Investment B increased 40% over six years.

The question is: which investment performed better?

It is not easy to answer this question directly, because the periods of the investments are different.

This is where a clever calculation, the compound annual growth rate (CAGR), can help us. The CAGR is a way of standardising investment performance to allow different investments to be compared with each other.

The CAGR is the theoretical annual growth rate of an investment.

In this case, the CAGR value for investment A is 5.5%. This tells us that investment A grew at an annual rate of 5.5% (to reach a total return of 45% over the seven years).

I won't go into the calculation here (that's what the internet is for) – it is not difficult, but is best calculated in a spreadsheet.

One way of thinking of a CAGR of 5.5% is to imagine inputting 100 (to represent starting capital of £100) into a calculator, and then multiplying that by 1.055 (to represent an annual return of 5.5%), the result will be £105.5 – the value of the investment after one year. Now hit the enter key on the calculator a further six times (to represent the investment growing at 5.5% for a further six years); the result will be £145 – making a total return of 45% (over the seven years).

The CAGR for investment B is 5.8%. Therefore we could say that the performance of investment B is superior to that of investment A as it has the higher CAGR.

Of course, in investing few things are ever completely simple. Here, it should be noted that the CAGR calculates a theoretical annual growth rate, which may be very different from the actual year-on-year performance. For example, although the CAGR of investment B is higher than A, it may be that investment B experienced greater volatility than A – meaning that in some years it delivered a lot less than 5.8%, and in some years it delivered a lot more – and may be less attractive as a result. We can't tell this from the CAGR.

However, putting the caveats aside, CAGR is still a very useful measure for standardising the measurement of investment performance because it allows the comparison of different investments over different time periods and also different asset classes. For example, it allows the annual returns from an equity investment to be compared with the return on cash in the bank.

We will be using this compound annual growth rate to compare the performance of different investments and investing strategies throughout the remainder of this book (and will refer to it as CAGR).

Comparing shares, bonds and cash using the concept of risk-adjusted returns

How can we compare the relative merits and drawbacks of each of these three asset classes – shares, bonds and cash – against each other?

The simplest and most effective method uses two variables: the level of investment return expected versus the level of financial risk taken. While investment returns can be pretty easily understood, I think it is worth taking a moment to consider the notion of financial risk – the first question being, how to define it?

You can then learn to appreciate and deal with your own comfort level with regards to investment risk, because this should be a prime determinant of your long-term investment outlook, and consequently of your own portfolio strategy.

Financial risk: the probability of getting less than you expect

Let's start with a simple definition of investment risk: the financial education website Investopedia defines financial risk as:

> The chance that an investment's actual return will be different than expected. Risk includes the possibility of losing some or all of the original investment.[6]

For any investor, the idea of knowing your own capacity for loss is a key determinant for which investments you will want to make later on.

---

6 www.investopedia.com is a useful US financial education website, which contains a whole section on financial definitions and also investing basics.

Observation 4

Knowing your own capacity for loss is an important first step in determining your ultimate investment strategy for your savings. But you need to be honest with yourself, as you will be kidding no-one but yourself ultimately!

In my view you should judge your own risk tolerance level first, before deciding on a target for an expected rate of return for your capital.

Taking greater risk for potentially greater reward

Why would any investor take greater risk when investing their capital? There must clearly be a reason.

Well, because there is a direct relationship between investment risk and investment returns – in general, low levels of uncertainty, or risk, are associated with low levels of investment return, while higher levels of uncertainty or risk are associated with higher returns.

So an investor takes greater risk when investing in the expectation of growing his or her capital faster. This makes sense – after all, if we were not compensated for the additional risk of holding shares over keeping our cash safe in the bank, then no one would ever own any shares, and companies would never have access to this shareholders' capital in the first place, which would be bad news for economic growth.

This is what is generally called the *risk-return trade-off* (Figure 5), and is a crucial concept in deciding your own personal investment strategy for your capital. The key here is for you to decide how much risk you are willing to take when investing your own capital for the long term, which will still allow you to sleep comfortably at night without worrying about any short-term gyrations in the value of your investments. This comfort level of investment risk will be very different for different people.

On the chart in Figure 5, imagine that cash held in a relatively risk-free savings account is somewhere on the bottom-left of this chart, while an investment in riskier shares would be somewhere at the top-right of the chart.

Figure 5: The risk/return trade-off

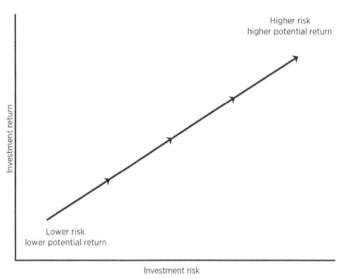

Demonstrating that shares are higher risk, higher reward, and cash lowest risk, lowest reward

Now, using actual investment risk and return data for the four major asset classes of shares (labelled UK equities), government bonds (UK gilts), property (UK housing) and cash, we can see the basic relationship between risk and reward has held true over the last 60 years (Figure 6). Both housing and gilts have proven more risky than cash but have given greater average returns over the period, while equities have performed best of all, but with a substantially greater risk exposure.

Figure 6: A basic layout of risk and reward for the four major asset classes

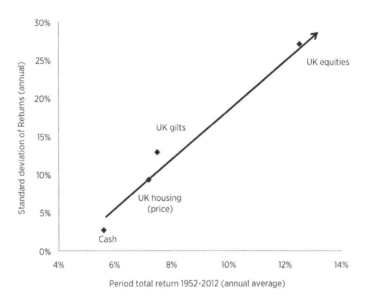

Source: Barclays Equity Gilt Study. Note: data for the 1952-2012 period.

Over the last 100 years (to 2012), UK shares have posted the best annual performance out of the three asset classes we are going to use some 55 times, so it has often been the best asset class to be invested in (Figure 7).

But clearly, there have also been 45 years (i.e. nearly half the time) where it has paid to be invested instead in bonds or cash, so a simple buy-and-hold strategy in shares will clearly not give the best long-term investment results.

Figure 7: Shares have performed best over 55 of the last 100 years

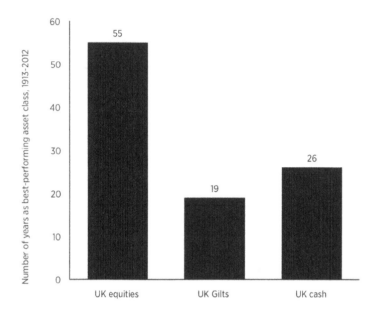

Source: Barclays Equity-Gilt Study.

Different assets perform well under different economic conditions

Shares have clearly given the best investment returns on average over the very long term; however, there are of course times when shares do very badly, typically when the UK and world economies are going into recession.

Looking at relatively recent history (the past 13 years), we can see that share markets suffered not one, but two crashes measuring a drop of over 50% in prices, and over 45% even including the offsetting influence of dividend payments (Figure 8).

Figure 8: UK shares saw peak-to-trough declines of nearly 50% in 2000-2 and 2007-9

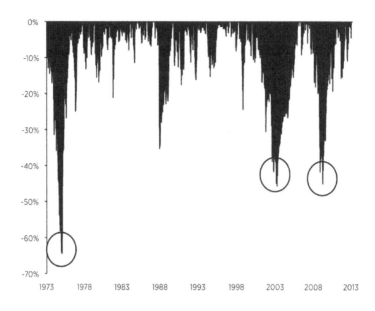

Source: Datastream; FTSE. Note: peak-to-trough calculations based on total return data (i.e. including dividends).

Government bonds tend to perform well when shares go down

Looking back to Figure 8, we can see that recessions over both 2000-02 and 2007-09 were very painful for investors in shares. Figure 9 points out the obvious, that investors did better off over these periods by instead being invested in government bonds (UK gilts) or cash.

So a first rule of thumb that we will use later in some of the Idle Investor strategies will be to invest in shares when they are in a general upwards trend (sounds obvious, right?), but then to switch out of shares and go into government bonds when share markets establish a falling trend.

In this way, we can capture the best of the long-term outperformance of shares, while side-stepping the bulk of the drawdowns in shares that can occur during bear markets (normally during economic recession) and even benefiting from the positive investment returns that government bonds usually post over these periods.

Figure 9: Better to be in bonds or cash when shares suffer

Years of equity market falls	UK equities total ret. (% y/y)	UK gilts total ret. (% y/y)	UK cash ret. (% y/y)
1920	-21.30%	-7.30%	6.10%
1929-31	-34.80%	10.70%	12.50%
1937-40	-24.00%	4.00%	3.70%
1969	-11.90%	0.00%	7.80%
1973-74	-64.10%	-22.70%	22.70%
1990	-9.60%	5.70%	15.90%
2000-02	-36.50%	20.30%	16.70%
2007-09	-29.80%	11.90%	5.20%

Source: Barclays Equity-Gilt Study. Note: calendar year total return data used.

Occasionally, shares and bonds go down together, and then cash is best

However, even this method of switching between shares and bonds is not foolproof; in 1973-74 for instance (see Figure 9), both shares and government bonds lost money owing to a (thankfully) rare combination of economic recession and stubbornly high inflation rates (inflation is generally bad news for government bonds as it erodes the after-inflation value of coupon payments).

At that point, cash savings actually performed much better than either shares or bonds, which is why we also need to keep the potential to invest in cash as a last resort should shares and bonds once again fall at the same time at some point in the future.

What is the best way to get exposure to shares and bonds?

How should we get our exposure to shares, and bonds, in the three investing strategies? Should we simply use a broad market index fund to take exposure to shares, or can we do better than that?

The advantages of using a broad market index-based fund like an ETF to buy exposure to shares are (a) ease, and (b) cheapness, as there are now many choices of broad stock market index fund that are available and which charge extremely low annual management fees, even under 0.1% per year.

However, there are a number of well-documented financial market effects that can be exploited using intelligent indices, which have over time proved to outperform the main benchmark share market indices. These market-beating financial market effects are the subject of the next chapter.

.

CHAPTER 5.

Beat The Share Market Without Breaking Sweat

*Using proven market anomalies to
your investment advantage*

Does the title of this chapter sound too good to be true?

Well, I have trawled through mounds of academic literature on the subject of factors that, when systematically used in an investment strategy, beat the overall stock market consistently over the long-term. This has enabled me to highlight five factors that can allow investors, applying these factors consistently to their investments, to beat the overall share market.

Five market-beating phenomena

The five market-beating phenomena that we are going to exploit later on in the three Idle Investor strategies are:

1. **Momentum:** shares that have already outperformed the overall share market tend to continue to outperform the market;

2. **Value:** cheap shares, as measured according to valuation ratios such as price/earnings or price/book value, tend to outperform both expensive shares and the share market;

3. **Size:** mid-cap and small-cap shares (such as the FTSE MID 250 and FTSE SmallCap indices) tend to outperform large-cap shares (such as the FTSE 100) in the medium to long run;

4. **Dividends:** shares that pay a consistent and higher than average dividend yield (dividend/share price) tend to outperform the stock market (as long as those dividends are reinvested in buying more of the same shares);

5. **Low Volatility:** shares that have smaller up- and down-variations in share price over time (known as *low volatility* shares) tend to give similar or better investment returns over time to those of the overall share market, but at a far lower level of investment risk. So the performance per unit of risk taken is far higher for these low volatility shares.

Let's now look at those five phenomena in some detail.

1. Momentum: what goes up generally keeps on going up

The momentum effect states that shares that have enjoyed strong price performance over the last 3 to 12-month period tend to continue to perform well over the subsequent 3 to 12 months.

Why this occurs is open to debate, with a number of differing explanations being offered. It frankly sounds a little bizarre that such a simple strategy should generate outperformance in different share markets around the world, but this has been shown to be the case by many different academics, including Jegadeesh and Titman with their paper 'Momentum'.[7]

---

7 N. Jegadeesh and S. Titman, 'Momentum', SSRN 299107 (2001).

In Europe the momentum effect seems to work particularly well, with Rouwenhorst showing that shares drawn from 12 different European share markets (including the UK, France, Germany and the Netherlands) which had performed strongest over the previous six months continued to outperform over the subsequent 3, 6, 9 and even 12 months, tested over the period 1980-1995. These shares posted about twice the average monthly price performance of the losers of the previous six months over these subsequent time periods. Figure 10 shows these results.

Figure 10: Average monthly buy-and-hold returns for momentum shares for a range of months following selection, 1980-1995

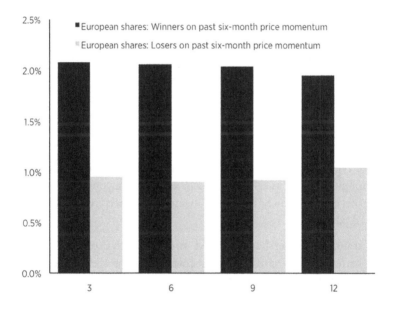

Source: K. Rouwenhorst (1998): International momentum strategies, *Journal of Finance* 53.

Figure 11 shows the use of this effect in the US share market from 1995 to 2013.

Figure 11: The momentum strategy beat the US stock market by 89% during 1995-2013

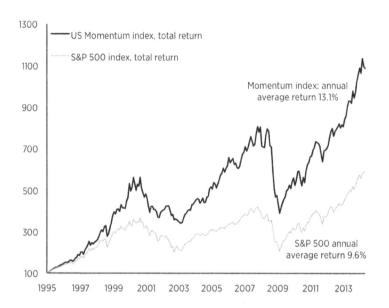

Source: Bloomberg.

One type of commonly-used investment strategy that exploits this momentum effect is called *trend-following*, where you invest in clear market trends that have already been established. According to a 2012 paper,

> trend-following has delivered strong positive returns and realized a low correlation to traditional asset classes each decade for more than a century.[8]

We will exploit this momentum effect in one of our long-term investment strategies by using momentum to select which index funds to buy in any given month, on the basis that those funds which have already done well should continue to do well for a number of further months.

---

8 Hurst, Ooi and Pedersen, 'A Century of Evidence on Trend-Following Investing' (2012).

2. Value: cheap and cheerful beats the market over the long haul

The value effect holds that cheap shares tend to outperform expensive shares over the medium to long term.

Shares that are classified as cheap or expensive have typically been measured on a number of traditional valuation criteria, including dividend yield (high is cheap), price/book (low is cheap), price/earnings (again, low is cheap), and so on. Famously, the billionaire investor Warren Buffett is a value investor following in the footsteps of Benjamin Graham, his mentor. Graham is often called 'the father of value investing' and he is author of *The Intelligent Investor*.

Fama & French looked at the performance of US shares sorted by value over 27 years from June 1963 to end-1990.[9] They demonstrated that value shares in the form of those with a low price/book ratio or a low price/earnings (P/E) ratio outperformed both the broad market, and in particular those shares ranked as expensive on the basis of price/book and P/E. Other studies have shown that this value effect is persistent through time, working consistently up until at least 2011 (e.g. Chaves & Arnott).[10] Figure 12 shows how the FTSE UK Value index beat the FTSE All-Share index in the period 1995 to 2013.

The outperformance of cheap shares (for instance, shares with a high dividend yield, low price/book ratios or low P/E ratios) over both expensive shares (with low dividend yields or high P/E ratios) and over the market as a whole has been documented over time by advocates of value-based share selection strategies. These include David Dreman (in *Contrarian Investment Strategies – The Next Generation*) and James O'Shaughnessy (*What Works on Wall Street*).[11]

---

9 E. Fama and K. French, 'The Cross-Section of Expected Share Returns', *The Journal of Finance* XLVII, No. 2 (1992).

10 D. Chaves and R. Arnott, 'Rebalancing and the Value Effect', SSRN 1982735 (2012).

11 D. Dreman, *Contrarian Investment Strategies – The Next Generation* (Simon and Schuster, 1998); J. O'Shaughnessy, *What Works on Wall Street* (McGraw-Hill, 2011).

Figure 12: Value beat the UK share market by 12% over 1995-2013

Source: FTSE, Bloomberg.

We will exploit this value effect later on in our long-term investment strategies via the use of value-based index funds.

3. Size: the best performance can come in smaller packets

Just as with value shares, smaller capitalisation shares have historically outperformed larger capitalisation shares over long periods of time.

This was a further factor identified by Fama & French as a significant determinant of a share's return over time (the others being the value effect and overall share market direction). From 1963 to 1980 in the US, for example, investing in the 10% of smallest market capitalisation shares consistently would have resulted in a cumulative return more than ten times greater than that for the largest shares! (See Figure 13.)

Figure 13: Small-cap shares outperform large-cap shares over time

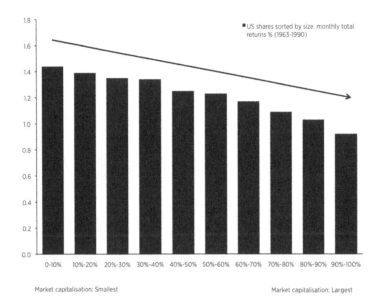

Source: Fama & French, 'The Cross-Section of Expected Share Returns', *The Journal of Finance* (1992).

In this book, we will compare the performance of the UK benchmark index, the FTSE 100, which comprises the largest 100 companies quoted in the UK (called large-caps), and other indices of UK shares that can capture the small-cap effect.

There are principally two such indices:

1. the FTSE MID 250 index, which comprises the 250 companies by size directly below the FTSE 100 index, and then

2. the FTSE SmallCap index, which comprises UK companies even smaller than those in the FTSE MID 250 index.

Both of these indices have been shown over time to capture this small-cap effect in outperforming the large-cap FTSE 100 by some distance. This is shown in Figure 14, where we can see that FTSE MID 250 stocks have generated 101% higher returns than the FTSE 100 since 1986.

Figure 14: Mid-cap shares have delivered twice the FTSE 100 return since 1986

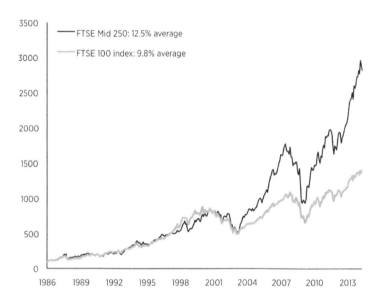

Source: FTSE.

There is a key advantage of the FTSE MID 250 index over the FTSE SmallCap index: this is better liquidity, which makes it generally easier and cheaper to trade. It is for this reason that one can easily find FTSE MID 250 index ETFs to buy, but not a true UK SmallCap ETF.

Therefore, in our investing strategies later in this book that exploit the small-cap effect, you will find that I have used FTSE 250 ETFs for this pragmatic reason.

Smaller-cap shares can be more volatile than large-cap shares over any short time period, so I would not necessarily advocate putting all your long-term investments into small-cap shares. However, in the long term the small-cap effect has proven to deliver superior investment returns and is thus worth trying to exploit via low-cost funds.

This is then a third effect that we will try to capture in our investment strategy, using smaller-cap index funds to get exposure to this effect while being careful to maintain sufficient liquidity (so that, for example, the buying and asking prices are not so far apart that a large amount of the effect is lost through costs).

4. Dividends: worth their weight in gold

Investors have generally tended to underestimate the significance of dividends over the long term, particularly when those dividends are systematically reinvested back into shares rather than being spent. In the UK, traditionally a higher-dividend paying stock market than the global average, higher dividend-paying shares (as measured in Figure 15 by the FTSE 350 Higher Yield index) have delivered a cumulative outperformance versus the benchmark FTSE 350 index of some 40% since 1986. On average, this represents annual outperformance of 1.3% per year – outperformance certainly worth having!

Figure 15: UK Higher Yield index has delivered 40% more than the FTSE 350 since 1986

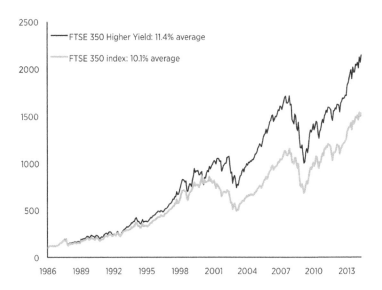

Source: FTSE.

This dividend bias is one we will exploit using dividend-focused index funds in our Idle Investor strategies.

5. Low volatility gives the best risk-adjusted performance

The low volatility effect refers to the anomaly that portfolios of low-volatility shares have produced higher risk-adjusted returns than portfolios with high-volatility shares in most markets studied. This goes contrary to what traditional financial market theory in the form of the Capital Asset Pricing Model (CAPM)[12] would predict. According to the CAPM, riskier assets should give greater returns, while in actual fact portfolios of low-volatility shares do consistently better than the CAPM would predict.

In the case of European shares, the S&P Europe Low Volatility index has beaten the broad European share market since 2002 by an impressively wide margin, delivering a compound average rate of return of 8.7% since 1998, compared with a compound annual average return of only 2.8% from the broad market index. This would turn an initial EUR100 into over EUR340 by the end of February 2013, compared with only EUR152 by end-February 2013 for the broad European share market. Figure 16 presents an illustration of this result.

In other words, you are better off in the long run investing in low-volatility, less risky shares as these will give you more investment return bang for your investment risk buck.

---

12 The Capital Asset Pricing Model is used to determine a theoretically appropriate required rate of return of an asset when added to an already-diversified portfolio based on its non-diversifiable level of risk.

Figure 16: European low volatility shares have beaten the market since 2000

Source: S&P Dow Jones Indices.

On to the shared elements of the three Idle Investor strategies

In the next chapter I will look at four elements that are shared by all three Idle Investor strategies: the compound interest effect, the power of diversification, the benefits of rebalancing, and the usefulness of using ETFs.

CHAPTER 6.

The Foundations Of The Three Idle Investor Strategies

The elements that are common to all three investment strategies

The key steps that are common to the three investment strategies outlined in this book are:

1. Applying a consistent **long-term investment strategy**, exposed to a large degree to the best-performing asset class of shares, in order to take advantage of the compound interest effect discussed in Chapter 2;

2. Buying funds in order to benefit from **diversification**;

3. Periodic rebalancing of investment portfolios to **manage financial risk**, and to avoid being exposed to unnecessary risk over time.

4. Using ETFs to keep **trading and management fees to a minimum**.

In the following pages, I will take you on a whistle-stop tour of these four steps and why they are important to our Idle Investor strategies. After that, we will get stuck into the strategies themselves.

1. What is the compound interest effect and why is it important?

"Compound interest is the eighth wonder of the world. He who understands it, earns it. He who doesn't pays it."

Albert Einstein

You don't have to be Albert Einstein to understand that compounding the return on any investment is an almost magic form of growing capital. Bizarrely enough, we are familiar with the power of compounding in certain financial subjects, namely house prices, but are not so good at thinking about other financial investments in these terms.

Getting away from the casino mentality in investing your own money is key to deriving the maximum benefit from the compounding effect. Do not expect to make large gains overnight, because that typically leads to overtrading and high risk-taking. This all tends to erode the beneficial compounding effect of a buy-and-hold strategy, where you try to buy the right investments for the long term in the beginning and stick with your judgment even when your investments suffer a bout of volatility (i.e. when they drop significantly in value because of the temporary whims and vagaries of financial markets).

The power of compounding at different rates

How powerful can the compound interest effect really be? Very powerful, is the short answer.

Figure 17 outlines the effect of compound interest over 40 years (a typical working lifetime) at different constant interest rates. Yes, I know that in practice this is never really the case, as interest rates typically vary over time, but humour me for now in this simple illustration.

Starting with a lump sum of £100 in year zero, look how each curve becomes more obviously exponential over time. At a 10% interest rate, for example, it takes just over seven years for this £100 to double, while it takes just nine years at an 8% rate. At a 6% rate, it takes 12 years, while at a 4% rate it takes just under 18 years.

Figure 17: The power of compounding, at different interest rates

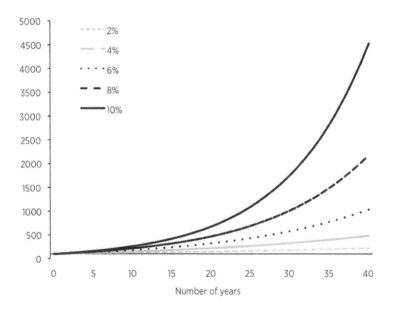

Number of years

Perhaps it would be a good idea to put these theoretical growth rates into more concrete pounds (no shillings or pence, though). The bar chart in Figure 18 shows the value of £100 compounded at a range of different interest rates from 2% per year to 10% p.a., over both 10 and 20 year spans.

Figure 18: Steady investing has its rewards, even after 10 years

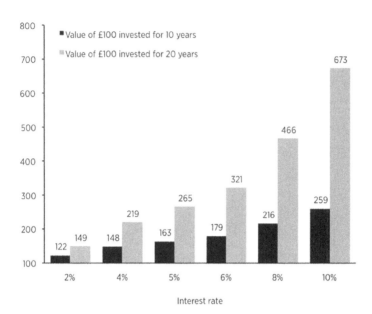

Interest rate

In the most extreme case, £100 that grows at a constant 10% p.a. turns into £259 after ten years, and an even more impressive £673 after 20 years – yet another striking illustration of the power of compounding in long-term investing.

Compounding reinvested dividends over time

One way that the power of compounding can be effectively harnessed in investing is via the systematic reinvestment of dividends back into shares. As an example of this power, I have taken UK share index data from the annual Barclays Equity-Gilt Study and compared the UK share market price index against an index where all dividends received are systematically reinvested back into shares.

First of all, let's look at the example where £100 is invested in UK shares in 1900 and see what happens by the end of 2012. First of all, the UK share market saw its price index move from 100 in 1900 to £12,753 by the end of 2012, a compound annual growth rate of 4.4% per year. On top of that, you would also have received a cumulative £9,330 in dividends paid out over the 112 years. If you had stuffed the cash dividends received every year under the mattress, you would have seen your £100 effectively turn into over £22,000 of shares and cash. A very nice return of 220 times your original investment, which is certainly nothing to sneeze at.

In a second example, let us instead assume that all dividends received are used each year to buy more exposure to UK shares, rather than being stuffed under the mattress. In this case, your £100 in shares in 1900 would have turned into over £1.8m by the end of 2012, a cumulative 112-year return of 18,000 times your original investment, all invested in UK shares. Rather more impressive, wouldn't you agree? This is the long-term power of compounding.

2. Diversification: a free lunch for your portfolio?

Diversification describes the mixing of different assets and asset classes within a single portfolio, with the express aim of reducing the overall risk of the portfolio while maximising the performance of that portfolio given the risk level chosen.

There are two basic types of diversification that I employ in the Idle Investor strategies to reduce risk while maintaining overall performance:

1. **Diversifying across many shares rather than just a few individual share holdings**, achieved using a number of shares-based ETFs that hold portfolios containing 50 or more shares each.

2. **Diversifying across different asset classes**, so not just holding 100% exposure to shares 100% of the time, but holding a dynamically diversified portfolio of asset classes mixing ETFs holding shares, ETFs holding a variety of bonds and also holding cash.

Can diversification really reduce overall investment risk? Yes!

Why should you not put all your eggs in one basket? Because if you drop this one basket, you risk breaking all your eggs, of course. The main argument in favour of diversifying the assets in your overall investment portfolio (i.e. holding different types of assets) is that it helps you to achieve a reduction in overall investment risk.

Sounds a good idea, doesn't it?

However, there is potentially a price to be paid for diversification in terms of the overall, long-term performance of an investment portfolio. So while diversification is an effective risk-reduction technique, there is a point at which further diversification beyond a certain point will worsen overall portfolio performance without delivering a further benefit in terms of lowering overall investment risk.

So, how is this reduction in investment risk via diversification actually achieved?

To illustrate the benefits of diversification for a buy-and-hold investor, I have constructed a comparison of equities, government bonds and cash using the annual total return data from 1899 to 2012 from the annual Barclays Equity-Gilt study.

Figure 19 gives risk and return statistics over the 113-year period for these three asset classes (as if an investor held their entire portfolios in one of these asset classes), plus a composite, diversified portfolio holding one-third of the overall portfolio each in UK equities, UK gilts and UK cash (assuming rebalancing of the portfolio every year to start each new year with the same one-third proportions invested in each asset class).

Figure 19: Risk and return statistics for UK investment 1899 to 2012, showing that simple diversification can achieve better returns with lower risk

Measure	100% UK equities	100% UK gilts	100% UK cash	33% each diversified
CAGR	9.10%	5.20%	4.80%	6.80%
Median total return (% y/y)	11.00%	3.60%	4.10%	5.90%
Volatility	21.80%	11.80%	3.80%	10.20%
Down years	27%	31%	0%	21%
Worst year	-50.20%	-20.30%	0.30%	-17.70%

Source: Barclays Equity-Gilt Study.

Interestingly, even the very simple diversified portfolio manages to simultaneously outperform a 100% UK gilts portfolio at lower levels of risk (21% of down years versus 31% for gilts, worst single year drawdown of 17.7% versus 20.3% for gilts). And when we compare the performance over the long-term, while of course the diversified portfolio cannot keep up with a 100% equities portfolio, it does manage to turn a starting £100 in 1899 into £162,573 by the end of 2012, compared with only £29,243 for the 100% UK gilts portfolio (see Figure 20).

Figure 20: Diversified portfolio beats bonds with lower risk, better returns

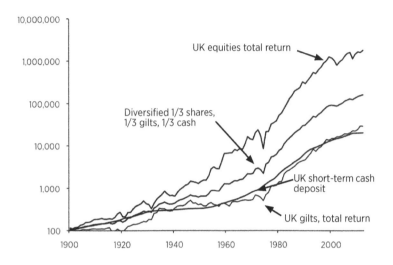

Source: Barclays Equity-Gilt Study. Note: logarithmic scale used.

3. Rebalancing portfolios: another way to reduce risk

Rebalancing is primarily about applying risk control to your investment portfolio over time, to ensure your portfolio isn't overly exposed to any single investment, asset class, or style at any given point. In order to ensure that your overall investment portfolio stays well diversified over time, periodic rebalancing of the portfolio back to the desired weightings in various asset classes is a good idea.

Let's take a simple example, that of a portfolio that we start at the beginning of 1990 with 50% invested in UK shares via a UK index fund (represented by the FTSE All-Share index), and 50% invested in UK gilts via a UK bond fund (represented by the FTSE UK gilts All Stocks index).

Case 1: No rebalancing at all

In this first case we just leave the initial investments alone over time. Including the compound effect of reinvested dividends and bond coupons, this 50:50 UK share and bond portfolio would have generated a CAGR (before fees) of 8.0%, taking £1000 invested at the beginning of 1990 to £6,286 by the end of 2013, at an annual volatility (a measure of risk) of 8.1%.

We can see from Figure 21 that as shares outperformed bonds, their weighting in the overall portfolio went up (to a maximum of 60%), and as they underperformed, their weighting went down (to a low of 40%). So there were quite a number of instances over the 24-year period when the portfolio weightings varied significantly from the original 50:50 split.

Figure 21: Share and bond weightings varied from 40%-60% over time

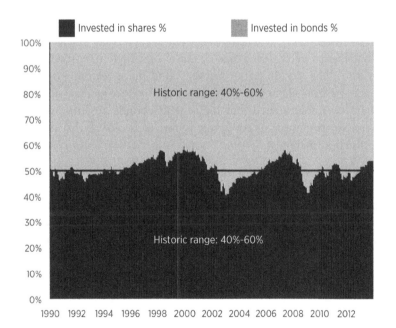

Source: FTSE.

Case 2: Annual rebalancing back to a 50:50 share:bond portfolio

In this second case, we make adjustments to the portfolio once per year. This effectively means that if shares outperform bonds in any given year, then at the moment of the annual rebalancing we will be selling some of the share fund position to finance the buying of an additional bond fund position, so as to return the share of each asset class in the overall portfolio to 50%. Generally, this involves one relatively small buy and sell trade each year, nothing more, so is only a slight increase in overall fees and costs for the portfolio.

However, introducing this annual rebalancing makes a significant difference to the performance of the overall portfolio. The CAGR (before fees) is now 8.3%, turning £1000 at the beginning of 1990 into £6,775 by the end of 2013, some 8% more than with the untouched share:bond portfolio (see Figure 22).

Secondly, this improvement in performance is achieved together with a lower level of volatility (investment risk), with average annual volatility of only 7.8% rather than the 8.1% in the non-rebalanced portfolio.

That regular rebalancing makes sense! No single investment style or asset class stays in favour forever. Bonds have been in vogue ever since the bear market of 2007-2009. In the bear market, nearly all shares were hammered, but high-quality bonds held up just fine. Since the beginning of 2009, shares have recovered all that they lost in the bear market.

And that's the whole point of rebalancing: you don't know what asset class, sector or investing style is going to rule the investment world next year, or how rapidly things might change. Rebalancing helps you reap the full rewards of diversification. Trimming back on a winner allows you to buy a laggard, protect your gains and position your portfolio to benefit from a change in the market's favourites.

Figure 22: Rebalancing added a cumulative 8% at lower risk

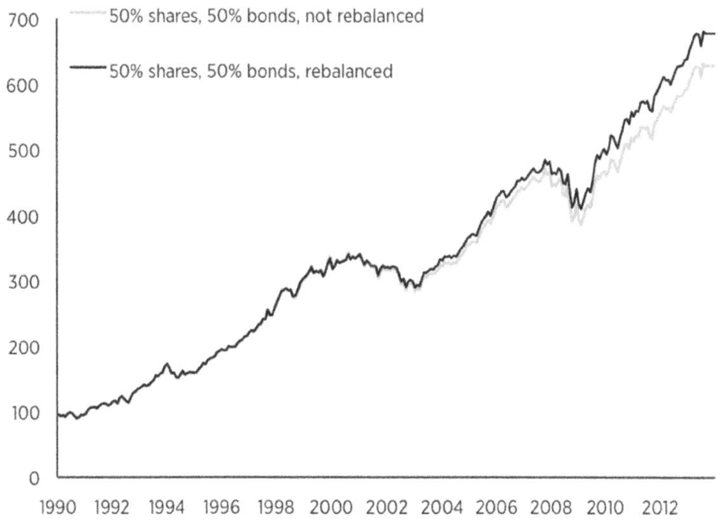

Source: FTSE.

What conclusion can we draw from this simple example?

How does this rebalancing improve investing performance over time?

Effectively, the rebalancing acts as a form of contrarian value strategy, taking a little capital out of the best-performing asset class each year, and putting it into the underperforming asset class.

In the original example above, for instance, equities outperformed bonds over the year to April, and thus at rebalancing time a small proportion of the outperforming equity fund was sold to increase the holding in the underperforming bond fund. This rebalancing done regularly thus adds a small value effect, which tends to boost the performance of the overall portfolio over time.

But how can we implement such a portfolio with two or more asset classes and annual rebalancing, in a simple, transparent and cost-effective manner? By using exchange-traded funds, of course.

4. What are exchange-traded funds and why use them?

I've mentioned ETFs a few times already; I'm assuming that you know the basics of what they are, but I'll summarise here a few of the main points about this type of fund.

Exchange-traded funds (ETFs):

1. **hold a broad portfolio of assets** (be they shares, bonds or even other assets like commodities), and

2. **are listed on a share exchange** so that they can be bought and sold during market opening hours (typically 8am to 4:30pm Monday to Friday in the UK, excluding Bank Holidays) just like any individual share.

There are several good reasons for using ETFs in our Idle Investor strategies:

1. **Low trading and management costs**: there is no stamp duty to pay, as there is when buying a share, and management fees can be even lower than 0.1% per year, so next to nothing. Trading costs start at around £7.50 per deal, and can rise to around £13 a deal with some brokers, which on a portfolio size of £10,000 or more is a very small cost.

2. **Ease of trading on a share exchange, with quoted live prices available at the time of trading**: you can choose whether to trade or not based on the prices you can see, which is not true, for instance, with unit trusts.

3. **Ever-broader choice of funds available from a wide variety of ETF providers**: you are not tied to just one fund provider, thus you have access to 'best of breed' funds.

4. **Flexibility to switch between these funds easily** even if held within a tax-efficient savings vehicle like an individual savings account (ISA) or self-invested personal pension (SIPP).

Now, we get to the exciting stuff – the Idle Investor strategies!

PART C.

3 Idle Investor Strategies

CHAPTER 7.

Investing Strategy 1: The Bone Idle Strategy

Limiting risk when investing in shares or other risky asset classes

The simplest of my three strategies presented is what I call the Bone Idle Strategy, as it involves very little work on the part of the investor.

For this strategy, you only need to do something to your portfolio either once or twice a year, as you prefer. The rest of the time, you can sit back and pursue your work or other interests, and leave these investments to hopefully grow steadily over time.

Remember too that by reinvesting all the dividends and interest you receive from the share and bond ETFs, plus the cash held for two months per year, you will benefit over time from the compound interest effect discussed previously.

In this chapter I will discuss the following key building blocks of the strategy:

1. Why the basis of this investing strategy is a 60% asset allocation to shares and 40% to bonds.

2. Adjustments to this basic asset allocation that can simultaneously improve the long-term investment returns and also reduce the risk taken, such as using a UK mid-cap share ETF for the share element of the strategy, and not staying invested in shares in September and October each year.

3. The actual returns and risk for the final seasonal asset allocation strategy.

4. How you can implement this investing strategy, step by step.

5. The pros and cons of this strategy.

6. Finally, there is an action plan at the end of the chapter to summarise all the steps in the investing process for this strategy.

Starting point: a basic asset allocation of 60% shares, 40% bonds

Let us return to the idea of using a simple mechanical system for investing. For those who want to do as little as possible regarding managing their own investments, I can propose a very simple, almost no-effort asset allocation system. This involves looking at your portfolio just *once* per year (in April) and not touching it the rest of the time.

Sounds just right for the archetypal Idle Investor, doesn't it?

How does it work? The basic principle is that we want to create a portfolio that is:

1. **Diversified by asset class** to limit the investment risk.

2. Able to benefit from good, or recovering, economic conditions through **exposure to risky assets like shares**, which will outperform in a growing economy.

3. **Exposed to lower-risk assets** like bonds to achieve the necessary diversification and reduced total investment portfolio risk.

OK, we are going to use just two asset classes for this system:

1. **Equities**: shares will be our higher-risk asset exposure to the order of 60%.

2. **Government bonds**: sovereign bonds will be our lower-risk asset exposure with an allocation of the remaining 40%.

Why a 60:40 asset allocation split between shares and bonds?

A 60:40 split between shares and bonds is a traditional asset mix often adopted in the US. The US index fund manager Vanguard has calculated that a portfolio of 60% in US shares and 40% in US bonds would have returned 8.6% on an annualised basis between 1926 and 2011, as compared to a more risky portfolio 100% invested in US shares, which would have returned 10.0% on average, but at the cost of far greater volatility. Not at all bad for a one-decision investing system!

As discussed before, we will use ETFs as our investment vehicle of choice (a) for simplicity, and also (b) in order to keep management costs as low as possible.

The strategy in practice

Follow this step-by-step approach:

1. Set up an account with a stockbroking service through which you can buy ETFs. This can be a bank, or an online stockbroker. I recommend the latter, as it is easier to keep track of your investments. The biggest providers of these online share broking services in the UK include *Hargreaves Lansdown*, *TD Direct* and *Barclays Stockbrokers* (details of their websites can be found in the Appendix).

2. You begin by deciding how much money you are going to invest for the long term. You then split this pot of investment capital into two portions, one of 60% that will be invested in an equity ETF and another of 40% that will be invested in a government bond ETF. So if you were to start with £1000 total investment capital, then £600 would be invested initially in an equity ETF and £400 would be invested in a government bond ETF.

3. Once per year, at the end of April, you need to perform a rebalancing exercise with the capital invested in the two funds, to re-establish the original 60:40 ratio between the capital invested in the equity and bond ETFs. This is a very basic form of risk control for the overall portfolio.

In the example below (Figure 23), £600 of the initial £1000 is allocated to invest into an equity ETF and £400 into a bond ETF. By end-April, the equity ETF has seen a price gain of 7%, growing the initial £600 to £642. In addition, it has also generated a dividend yield of 3%, or an additional £18 in income. So the equity ETF overall has delivered a total return of £60, growing the initial £600 to £660.

Figure 23: Simple asset re-allocation example

Capital in £	Equity ETF	Bond ETF	Total
Start (£)	600	400	1,000
End-April			
Price gain (£)	42	12	
Income (£)	18	8	
Total end-April (£)	660	420	1,080
Asset ratio	60%	40%	
New allocations (£)	648	432	1,080
Action required	-12	12	

The bond ETF has also seen a modest level of price growth (3%), taking the initial £400 to £412. To this we can add the bond coupon worth some 2% on top, or an additional £8. Overall, then, the bond ETF has generated a £20 total return, taking the total capital to £420. The two ETFs together have thus grown the original £1000 invested to £1080.

We then re-allocate this £1080 investment pot according to the original 60:40 ratio between the equity and bond ETF, suggesting that we should have £648 (60% of £1080) invested in the equity ETF and £432 (40% of £1080) invested in the bond ETF.

To achieve this we need to sell £12 of the equity ETF and reinvest this amount into the bond ETF. And that is it! Nothing then needs to be done until the following April, when the process is repeated.

How did this strategy perform in the past?

In the UK, since the beginning of 1990, this 60:40 rebalanced equities/bonds strategy generated a CAGR of 8.5% (before costs), turning £100 at the start of 1990 into £639 by the end of 2012 (see Figure 24).

This performance bettered that of both UK shares (8.3% CAGR 1990-2012) and UK government bonds (8.0% CAGR). Clearly, from the long-term investor's viewpoint, the higher CAGR the better.

Figure 24: The 60:40 share:bond strategy outperformed the UK share market, but with less volatility

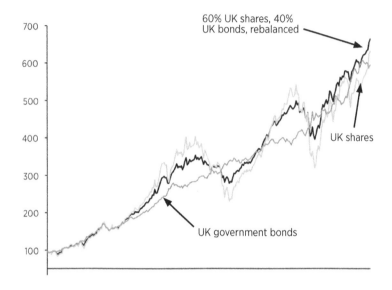

Source: Thomson Reuters Datastream. Note: all values are based on total return data.

Enhancement 1: Using a UK mid-cap share fund

One way to boost the performance of this 60:40 asset strategy is to replace the UK shares component with a UK mid-cap equity fund, thus introducing the so-called small-cap effect into the performance equation.

Recall that, according to the small-cap effect discussed earlier, smaller-cap companies tend to outperform large-cap companies over the medium to long term. We can take advantage of this effect by substituting the UK equities ETF with a UK mid-cap fund. Over the long-term, mid-caps have been the best performers by size, handily outperforming FTSE 100 large-cap shares.

Why not use a small-cap fund, I hear you ask?

For two simple reasons: firstly, in the UK, the FTSE MID 250 index has historically outperformed even the FTSE SmallCap index over the long term. Secondly, there are a number of liquid FTSE 250 index ETFs available, while there are no equivalent UK small-cap ETFs (you would have to resort to using small-cap investment trusts, which would be more costly).

The performance of this enhanced 60:40 strategy is shown in Figure 25. At the cost of a slightly higher level of volatility, notably over the 2007-09 bear market when this mid-cap shares/bonds strategy underperformed the original 60:40 share-bond strategy, the performance of this mid-cap 60:40 strategy is significantly better.

The mid-cap version delivered a CAGR of 9.4% (versus 8.5% for the original 60:40 strategy), turning £100 in 1990 into £760 by the end of 2012. This is some £121 more than in the original 60:40 strategy.

Figure 25: UK mid-cap 60:40 strategy does better still

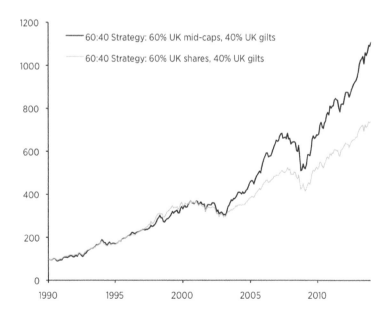

Source: Thomson Reuters Datastream. Note: all values are based on total return data.

Enhancement 2: Avoid the worst months of the year for shares

Another improvement that we can add easily to this 60:40 strategy is to make use of the calendar. There are persistent seasonal effects that have been observed over time in all major developed share markets.

Avoiding share market exposure in the most volatile months of September and October (the two months when share market crashes have typically occurred in the past) would have improved the performance of the diversified 60:40 strategy yet further, as can be seen in Figure 26.

Figure 26: Avoiding the worst months of the year for shares enhances the 60:40 strategy

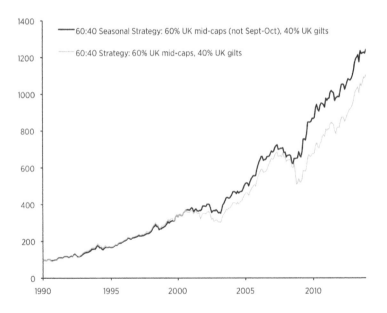

Source: Thomson Reuters Datastream. Note: all values are based on total return data.

Translating all of this into CAGRs for the period 1990-2012 gives the results shown in Figure 27 for the three varieties of 60:40 share:bond allocation strategies.

Figure 27: CAGRs for the three varieties of the 60:40 strategy

60% UK shares/40% gilts	60% UK mid-caps/40% gilts	60% UK mid-caps (not Sept-Oct)/40% gilts
8.70%	10.50%	11.00%

Source: Thomson Reuters Datastream. Note: all values are based on total return data, 1990-2012.

Now, while the performance of the diversified 60:40 asset allocation portfolio looks relatively steady, there were still significant drawdowns over the last two serious bear markets in 2002-03 and 2007-09. Even so, each of the three 60:40 portfolios outperformed a buy-and-hold share strategy handsomely thanks to the 40% of the portfolio allocated to government bonds, which performed consistently well over these periods.

Figure 28 highlights that the seasonal diversified 60:40 portfolio would have managed to limit the drop in portfolio value during the 2000-2003 bear market to 8% and the drop during the 2007-2009 financial crisis was limited to 14%, compared with a fall in the value of UK and European benchmark share indices of up to 50%.

So our first Idle Investor investing strategy is born: a 60:40 share:bond asset allocation portfolio that makes use of both the small-cap and seasonal effects in order to improve both the investment returns and investment risk exposure of the basic 60:40 share:bond index portfolio.

85

Figure 28: UK portfolio ex-September-October limits downside

Period	60% UK shares/40% gilts	60% UK mid-caps/40% gilts	60% mid-caps (not Sept-Oct)/ 40% gilts
Sept 2000– Mar 2003 (at worst)	-21%	-18%	-8%
June 2007– Mar 2009 (at worst)	-19%	-25%	-14%

Source: Thomson Reuters Datastream. Note: all values are based on total return data, 1990-2012.

Investing Strategy 1: The Bone Idle Strategy

For those who want the minimum of fuss in managing their own investments, and who are prepared to look through a little turbulence in the portfolio in times of recession or crisis, the seasonal diversified 60:40 portfolio is a good, simple, low-maintenance strategy.

You simply have to follow these steps:

1. **Divide starting capital into 60% and 40% proportions**: Take your starting investment capital, which can be held within a shares ISA, a share dealing account or even a self-invested personal pension, and divide it up two amounts: 60% to be allocated to a share ETF, and 40% to a bond ETF.

2. **Invest in a share ETF and a bond ETF**: Assuming that you are not starting to follow this investing system in September or October (I recommend starting at the beginning of the year or at the beginning of a new tax year if investing via an ISA), then you invest the 60% share portion into the following exchange-traded fund:

- iShares FTSE 250 ETF (code: MIDD)

and the 40% portion into the

- Vanguard UK Government Bond ETF (code: VGOV)

(Note, similar ETFs from different providers such as State Street, Powershares, Lyxor and Deutsche Bank x-trackers are also available.)

If you are starting in September or October, then you will only invest initially in the bond ETF and will leave the 60% share portion of your capital in cash to begin with.

In this way, you will end up with an initial allocation of 60% of your capital to shares and 40% to bonds (unless starting in September or October, in which case you will have 40% in bonds and the remaining 60% in cash).

3. **Leave both ETFs invested until the end of August:** there is nothing further to do until the end of August. So you can get on with the many other preoccupations in life without worrying about these investments.

4. **Beginning of September, sell the share ETF:** At the beginning of September, we apply our seasonal risk reduction strategy by selling the mid-cap share ETF and leaving the proceeds in cash until the end of October.

5. **Beginning of November, buy back the mid-cap share ETF:** By the beginning of November, the statistically most dangerous period of the year for share markets is past and so you use the cash balance in your account (including any dividends and interest received over the prior 12 months) to buy the UK mid-cap ETF.

6. **End-April, rebalance the two ETFs (if necessary):** As a further risk reduction measure, at the end of April you should adjust your holdings in the two ETFs in your portfolio so that the mid-cap share ETF represents 60% of your total portfolio and the UK bond ETF represents 40% of the value of your total portfolio. This is likely to involve the buying and selling of small amounts of each ETF to bring them all back into balance. However, I wouldn't be over-zealous on this point, as this will involve trading costs (the commission on the buying and selling, plus the bid-ask

price difference for each ETF). So to avoid any unnecessary cost, I would only rebalance the portfolio if one ETF has performed far better than the other, resulting in the share ETF representing either more than 65% or less than 55% of your total portfolio at end-April.

And that is it, six steps involving intervening in your investment portfolio a mere twice or three times per year, and leaving your investments completely alone from the beginning of November to the end of August each year (if you don't wish to rebalance the portfolio at end-April – see point 6 above for why you may choose not to).

Following these few steps in the 60:40 investment process, you should comfortably beat most mixed asset allocation funds over time, with reduced investment risk, lower costs and little personal effort.

The 60:40 split

There is no reason why the 60:40 split employed by this strategy could not be more in favour of shares if you are willing to tolerate more volatile movements in the value of your investment portfolio, or indeed more in favour of bonds if you want to be more conservative and limit risk more.

You could for instance go with a more aggressive, higher allocation to shares and a lower allocation to bonds (e.g. 70% to equities and only 30% to bonds), as a way of boosting long-term returns, particularly if you are younger, being a long way from retirement, and thus feel able to take on a very long investment horizon.

But there is no free lunch here: the exposure to potentially higher long-term returns is obtained at the cost of higher investment risk to the overall portfolio.

The Bone Idle Strategy (1): Pros and Cons

First of all, let's examine the pros of this first Idle Investor system:

1. There are only two investment funds you need to buy and they can both be bought easily.

2. You achieve a relatively balanced, diversified portfolio straightaway, without needing to go to the effort of trying to figure out what a good fund is.

3. For nine or ten months of the year, you have absolutely nothing to do, just let the investments do their work.

4. You only have to sell the mid-cap share ETF once at the end of August and then buy it back again at the end of October.

5. You only have to rebalance the funds so as to retain a 60:40 ratio between share and bond ETFs once per year at the end of April, and even then, only if the share ETF proportion of the total portfolio has risen above 65% or fallen below 55%.

6. The combination of 40% in bonds plus avoiding share exposure for the months of September and October each year simultaneously boosted investment returns over a static 60% UK shares:40% UK bonds portfolio and also reduced the fall in portfolio value over the 2001-2003 recession and the 2007-2009 financial crisis.

7. Transaction costs are low – I estimate 0.3% per year for switching the share ETF into cash for two months per year and then back into the share ETF. To this you need to add the annual management fees for holding the ETFs, which is around 0.2% per year. So overall costs for running this strategy are 0.5% per year, which is pretty low for the performance that this strategy has seen historically.

However, there are a few cons to this investing system too:

1. You have to be prepared to be patient at times of recession and crisis. For instance, over the 2007-2009 financial crisis, this system took over two years to recover to the pre-crisis high point touched in early 2007, so short-term investment returns are certainly not guaranteed, while there is always investment risk.

2. There are some years where the months of September and October can provide very good share market returns, with an average +2.1% return from the UK share market over these two months between 1990 and 2012 (see Figure 29), so it seems a shame to throw the baby out with the bathwater and simply avoid any share market exposure over those two months each year.

Figure 29: Average +2.1% return from UK shares over September-October from 1990 to 2012

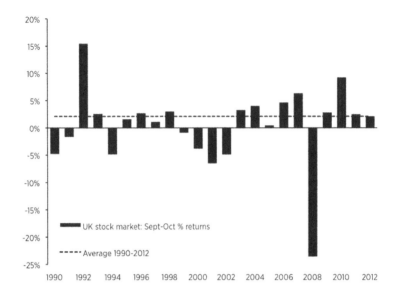

Source: Thomson Reuters Datastream. Note: all values are based on total return data.

Action Plan: Strategy 1 – The Bone Idle Strategy

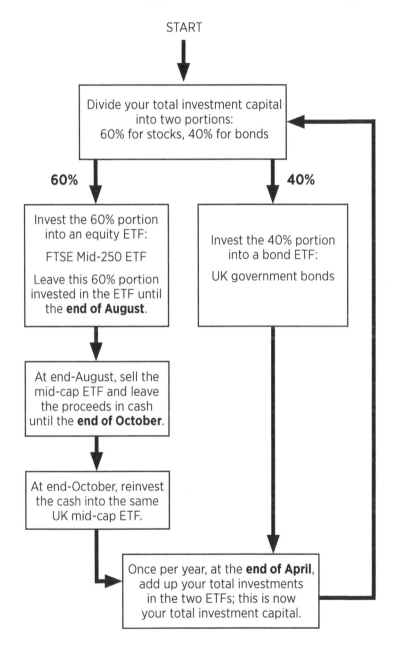

START

Divide your total investment capital into two portions:
60% for stocks, 40% for bonds

60%

Invest the 60% portion into an equity ETF:

FTSE Mid-250 ETF

Leave this 60% portion invested in the ETF until the **end of August**.

40%

Invest the 40% portion into a bond ETF:

UK government bonds

At end-August, sell the mid-cap ETF and leave the proceeds in cash until the **end of October**.

At end-October, reinvest the cash into the same UK mid-cap ETF.

Once per year, at the **end of April**, add up your total investments in the two ETFs; this is now your total investment capital.

Summary

Asset allocation	1. UK government bonds 2. UK mid-cap shares 3. Cash
Idleness indicator (frequency of action required)	Twice per year: 1. At the beginning of September (sell share ETF). 2. At the beginning of November (buy share ETF). Remember at the beginning of November to reinvest any dividends you have received over the previous 12 months, 60% in the shares ETF and 40% in the bond ETF. Optional third action to take at end-April each year to rebalance the proportions of your capital held in the share and bond ETFs to the 60%:40% proportions, if the proportions in each ETF are more than 5% away from these proportions.
Investing principles	1. Diversify by holding a mixture of shares, bonds, cash. 2. Invest in shares for long-term growth. 3. Invest in bonds for income and lower risk. 4. Invest in cash for lower risk.
Investing strategy	Seasonal: Avoiding shares in September and October, which are statistically the worst months for UK shares.
Asset split (January–August; November–December)	60% equities 40% bonds
Asset split (September and October)	60% cash 40% bonds
Long-term performance (compound annual growth rate)	11.0% CAGR (1990-2012)
Risk (worst fall peak-to-trough)	2007-2009: -14%

CHAPTER 8

Investing Strategy 2: The Summer Hibernation Strategy

"The genius of investing is recognizing the direction of a trend – not catching highs and lows."

John Bogle

Making more aggressive use of seasonal effects in financial markets

The next of the Idle Investor strategies is what I call the Summer Hibernation Strategy, as it employs a more aggressive form of seasonal investing – buying and holding higher-risk, higher-return shares via a variety of share ETFs for seven months per year (winter and spring) with 100% of your investment capital, but then buying and holding a selection of government bond ETFs instead with 100% of your capital over the summer and autumn months (five months per year). This is akin to your capital hibernating over the summer period each year.

You only need to do anything to this portfolio twice a year: once at the beginning of May, and once at the beginning of November.

Once again, note that by reinvesting all the dividends and interest you receive from the share and bond ETFs when you shift from bonds into shares at the beginning of November and again when you shift back into bonds from shares at the beginning of May each year, you will benefit over time from the compound interest effect.

In this chapter I will discuss the following key building blocks of this strategy:

1. Why the basis of this seasonal investing strategy is a 100% asset allocation either to share ETFs or to bond ETFs, determined by the month of the year.

2. The actual returns and risk for the final seasonal asset allocation strategy.

3. How you can implement this investing strategy, step by step.

4. The pros and cons of this strategy.

5. Finally, there is an action plan at the end of the chapter to summarise all the steps in the investing process for this strategy.

Problems with the Bone Idle 60:40 shares:bonds strategy

As good as the 60:40 strategy we looked at in Chapter 7 is, there are two problems with it.

Problem 1: the 60:40 asset allocation portfolio still got hurt in the last two bear markets

Using the seasonal share/bond 60:40 asset allocation strategy described in the previous chapter may have lessened the impact of the last two bear markets (2000-03 and 2007-09), but it did not eliminate them by any means (as can be seen in the falls in portfolio value shown in Figure 28).

The cost of doing basically nothing for ten months of the year with this strategy would have meant suffering a drawdown in the investment portfolio of 14% from June 2007 to March 2009, even with 40% of the portfolio in bonds and the remaining 60% in cash rather than shares for the months of September and October each year.

Problem 2: it is unlikely to keep up its performance, given low bond yields

The second potential problem is the level of government bond yields at the time of writing. With long-term bond yields now close to the lowest that they have been since 1950, the 30-year bond bull market that we have enjoyed looks now to be over. So the CAGR from UK gilts of 10.6% from 1980 to 2012 seems unlikely to be repeated going forwards. Future returns from government bonds will likely be far lower than the high historical average of 10.6% achieved annually since 1980 (see Figure 30).

If bond returns were to return to their 1900-1950 average, when bond yields last sat within the 2%-4% range, then we can look forward to average returns closer to 3% per year, rather than the double-digit average returns that we have benefited from between 1980 and 2012 as long-term interest rates fell from a peak of over 13% to under

3% today (remember, bond prices increase as bond yields decline, generally as inflation rates fall).

Clearly, if government bonds are to yield closer to 3% in future rather than the 10% to 11% that we have enjoyed over the past 32 years, then any asset allocation strategy that keeps 40% in bonds is not going to perform as well in future as it has done in the past, given the absence of this following wind from bond markets.

Figure 30: Future bond returns could return to 1900-1950 levels

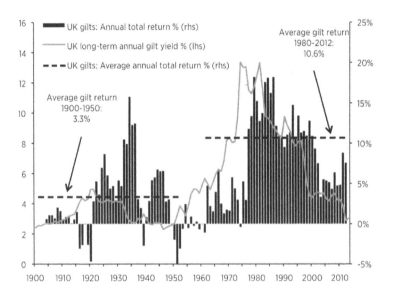

Source: Barclays Capital, Bank of England.

Timing strategies: seasonal effects

The Bone Idle investing strategy benefits from a limited form of seasonal effect, in that it avoids investing in UK shares over September and October, when returns from shares have been poorest historically.

This Summer Hibernation strategy makes more aggressive use of the seasonal effect that has been reliably demonstrated in many share and bond markets around the world over history, and encapsulated in studies of the Halloween Effect and in the old stock market adage 'Sell in May and Go Away'.

It has been noted in academic studies that there are a number of seasonal effects at play in financial markets, whose effects have been relatively persistent over time. For example, since 1974 there has been a clear seasonal difference at play in equities; this is the famous January effect whereby small-cap shares tend to outperform large cap shares in January.[13]

Another seasonal effect is demonstrated in Figure 31, where investing in UK equities from the beginning of November to the end of April each year, and then switching into cash for the remaining six months, has delivered consistently higher returns than the index, particularly since 2000.

---

13   Haugen and Jorion, *Financial Analysts Journal* (1996).

Figure 31: Holding shares over November to April has given best results

Source: Thomson Reuters Datastream.

The chart shows that investing in the UK share market from the beginning of November each year to the end of April the following year, and then selling out to keep capital in a cash deposit account until the following November, has generated a CAGR of 11.2%. In contrast, running the opposite strategy (i.e. being invested in the UK share market only from May to October) has yielded a simply dreadful 0.5% CAGR!

Seasonal effects also evident in Europe, the US and emerging markets

Performing the same analysis on other equity markets yields similar results. In the UK, the seasonal effect has been especially strong since 1974. From 1990, the November-April seasonal strategy has also worked well in Germany, MSCI Emerging Markets and the US. Indeed, in the emerging markets the seasonal effect is especially pronounced, achieving the best absolute and risk-adjusted returns since 1995.

In all cases and over different time periods (1990-2012 and 1974-2012), the seasonal investing approach yields a higher total return at lower volatility than the classic equities buy-and-hold strategy.

In the case of small-cap shares, the seasonal effect tends to extend from the beginning of November to the end of May, adding an extra month's-worth of share market exposure. This is shown in Figure 32.

Figure 32: Small-caps have performed best over December-May

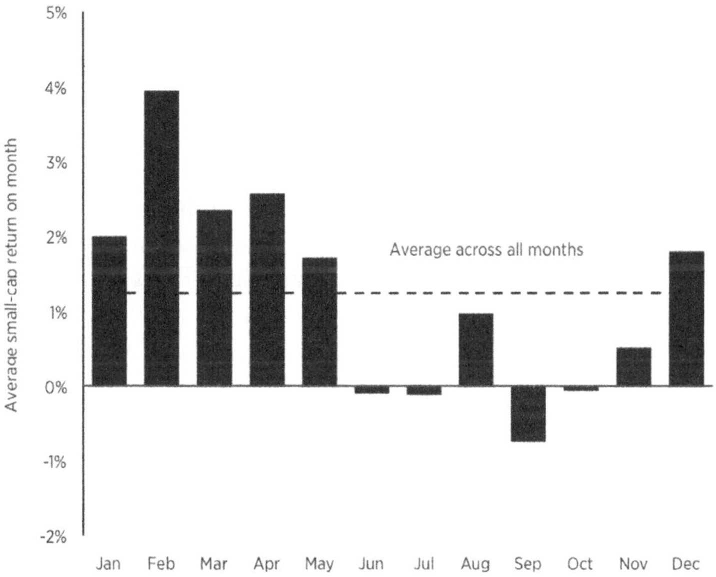

Source: Thomson Reuters Datastream. Note: Monthly UK Small-Cap index returns 1973-2012.

The summer hibernation strategy: step-by-step

And so to our second investing strategy: The Summer Hibernation Strategy.

Here, in contrast to the first seasonal diversified 60:40 share:bond strategy, we instead hold 100% exposure to either shares or bonds at any point. In this case, the diversification is done through time rather than via an asset allocation mix.

Effectively, over 12 months this second strategy is invested in shares 58% of the time (7 months out of 12), and 42% of the time in government bonds (5 months out of 12). Over the calendar year this is actually quite close to the 60:40 shares:bonds allocation in Strategy 1. But the greater element of investment risk is taken over the winter months by investing in shares, while in the summer months from May to October, the strategy takes a hibernation approach by investing instead in lower-risk government bonds.

So, how do we invest according to this seasonal strategy?

Step 1: Hold share exposure for seven months: For the seven-month period from the beginning of November to the end of May, we invest in a combination of three share-based ETFs to give some degree of geographic diversification:

1. UK mid-caps (iShares FTSE 250 ETF, code: MIDD),

2. European low volatility (iShares MSCI Europe Minimum Volatility ETF, code IMV), and

3. US small-cap (iShares S&P SmallCap 600 ETF, code ISP6).

Step 2: Then sell share exposure and instead buy bond exposure for five months: At the beginning of June each year, we then sell 100% of these three share ETFs and with the proceeds buy 100% into three government bond ETFs, which are then held for the remaining five months until the end of October:

1. UK gilts (Vanguard UK Government Bond ETF, code VGOV),

2. Euro government bonds (iShares Core Euro Government Bond ETF, code SEGA), and

3. US government bonds (iShares US Aggregate Bond ETF, code SUAG).

At the beginning of November, sell the three bond ETFs and reinvest the resulting cash in equal amounts into the three share ETFs in step 1.

And that is about all you need to do for this second investing strategy.

The results of this seasonal strategy applied over the 23 years from 1990 to 2012 are shown in Figures 33 and 34.

Figure 33: A seven-month shares, five-months bonds seasonal approach

	Strategy 2: seven months 100% mixed shares, five months 100% mixed bonds	Strategy 1: 60% UK mid-cap shares, 40% bonds, seasonal cash	Benchmark: 60% UK shares, 40% UK bonds
CAGR	15.20%	11.00%	8.60%
Worst drawdown (2008-09)	-22%	-14%	-21%

Note: transaction costs included at 0.25% per switch between share and bond ETFs.

Even after estimated transaction costs of 0.25% per switch between share and bond ETFs (which occurs twice per year), this seven-month shares, five-months bonds strategy would historically have delivered an average return of over 15% per year, nearly 5% per year better than the first modified 60% shares:40% bonds strategy.

Figure 34: Seven months in shares, five months in bonds has worked
well

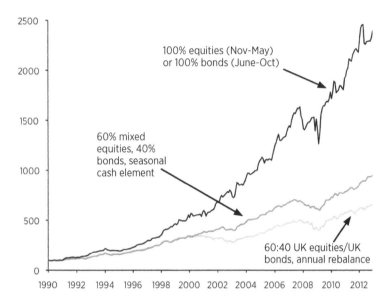

Source: Thomson Reuters Datastream. Note: Seasonal equities/bonds
strategy is invested in three share indices from beginning of November to
the end of May each year, and in three bond indices from the beginning of
June until the end of October.

However, there is a cost to this additional performance, in the form
of heavier setbacks to portfolio values at times of severe recession or
crisis. Over the period 2007-2009 this seasonality strategy would
have lost some 22% from pre-crisis peak-to-trough in early 2009,
more than would have been the case for the Bone Idle Strategy, which
would have only lost 14% over the same period.

The summer hibernation strategy (2): pros and cons

There are a number of reasons that a slightly less idle Idle Investor would use this second Idle Investing system rather than the first strategy described in the previous chapter:

- Long-term performance has been substantially better by nearly 5% per annum – and compounded up over a number of years, that makes a huge difference to long-term investment portfolio performance – over 1990-2012, this translated into a doubling of portfolio performance.

- You could argue that this system is even easier than the first strategy in practical terms, in the sense that you only have to execute two sets of buy and sell orders twice per year at the beginning of every November and May in order to switch 100% of the portfolio between share and bond ETFs. Notably, with this strategy there is no annual rebalancing to be done between the shares and bond allocation, as at any point in time the portfolio is 100% allocated to one or the other.

- However, there are drawbacks with this second Idle Investor portfolio too, most notably that this Summer Hibernation Strategy suffers more from recessions and crises than the Bone Idle strategy – this is the counterparty to the better long-term investment returns – so this second Idle Investor strategy may require a slightly stronger stomach over time.

Controlling for downside risk: using market timing signals

While the Summer Hibernation Strategy has worked very well over the last 20-odd years, we cannot ignore the fact that it still suffers relatively long periods where it either loses money or stalls. The 15% drawdown over 21 months during the 2007-2009 financial crisis would test the resolve of just about any investor, retail or professional.

So while these figures are still nothing like the losses suffered by a 100% equities-exposed buy-and-hold investor, I nevertheless wanted to explore whether there was a way of maintaining the positive long-term investment performance trend, while limiting the drawdowns even further and thus improving risk-adjusted performance. To this end, I examine the use of mechanical market timing signals in the next chapter as a way of achieving even better performance at lower levels of investment risk, known in portfolio management parlance as *better risk-adjusted performance from asset allocation.*

Action Plan: Strategy 2 – the summer hibernation strategy

Note that this second investing system only requires reallocating of the portfolio 100% between three share ETFs and three bond ETFs twice per year, at the beginning of June (from shares to bonds) and again at the beginning of November (from bonds back into shares). At these two asset switching moments, the three portions invested in shares or bonds should be divided so as to be equal when the switch is made.

The action plan is shown on the next page.

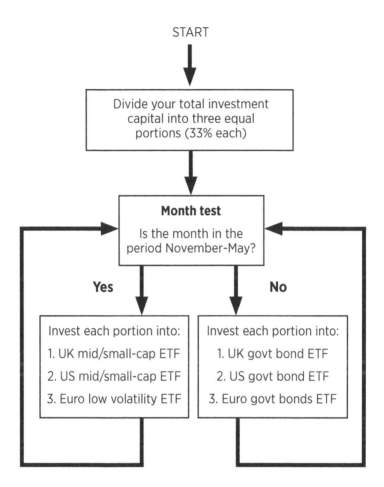

START

Divide your total investment capital into three equal portions (33% each)

Month test

Is the month in the period November-May?

Yes

No

Invest each portion into:

1. UK mid/small-cap ETF

2. US mid/small-cap ETF

3. Euro low volatility ETF

Invest each portion into:

1. UK govt bond ETF

2. US govt bond ETF

3. Euro govt bonds ETF

Return to month test and repeat every month

Summary

Asset allocation	1. Three share ETFs: UK mid-caps, US small-caps, European low volatility. 2. Three government bond ETFs: UK gilts, US treasuries, Eurozone government bonds.
Idleness Indicator **(frequency of action required)**	Twice per year: 1. At the beginning of May (sell three share ETFs and buy three bond ETFs in equal measure). 2. At the beginning of November (buy three share ETFs in equal measure and sell 3 bond ETFs). Remember at the beginning of May and November to reinvest any dividends you have received since the previous asset re-allocation (the prior November or May respectively), 100% in the share ETFs or 100% in the Bond ETFs depending on the period.
Investing principles	1. Diversify over time by holding shares for seven months per year and bonds for five months per year. 2. Invest in shares for long-term growth. 3. Invest in bonds for income, lower risk.
Investing strategy	Seasonal: Holding shares from November to April when share returns have historically been highest, and instead holding government bonds from May to September when they have traditionally delivered better risk-adjusted returns than shares.
Asset split (November-April)	100% equities
Asset split (May-October)	100% bonds
Long-term performance (compound annual growth rate)	15.2% CAGR (1990-2012)
Risk (worst fall peak-to-trough)	2007-2009: -22%

CHAPTER 9

What Mechanical Investing System Works Best?

Sifting through academic studies to find the system that delivers best performance at lowish risk

So far, we have examined two mechanical investing strategies that have proven to work well over time, and which do not require much ongoing effort on the part of the investor – except, of course, to follow the prescribed investment course as instructed, and not to deviate from the strategy even when results may temporarily take a dip.

Before launching into a detailed description of my third Idle Investor strategy, let's review what we are looking for in an ideal mechanical investment system:

1. Can be operated at most once per month, not requiring a large investment of time from the investor (so as to qualify as suitable for an *Idle Investor*).

2. Does not require any special knowledge on the part of the investor and can be operated on the basis of information that is freely available on the internet.

3. Delivers relatively consistent investment returns, even if these returns are not enormous in any particular year – consistency and avoiding large *drawdowns* (investment losses) is more important.

4. Limits downside risk in case of bear markets in shares (e.g. 2000-03 and 2007-09).

5. Contains sufficient diversification into different asset classes to spread investment risk away both from a single geography (e.g. just the UK) and away from a single asset class (e.g. just bonds or just shares).

6. Uses low-cost funds for investment, readily available on a low-cost, execution-only trading platform, thereby limiting overall costs to the investor and preserving investment returns.

This may sound like a very tall order to achieve, but I believe that the third Idle Investor strategy I present in the next chapter satisfies all of the above criteria!

Going one better: using academic studies on asset allocation

A good place to start in our hunt for better investment performance from a mechanical investing system is in the academic literature surrounding the optimising of risk and reward in asset allocation. There is plenty of such literature that one can wade through, but I will spare you the gory details. I can basically summarise two key studies by Faber[14] and Clare et al.[15] as follows: trend-following is a

14 M. Faber, Cambria Investment Management, 'A Quantitative Approach to Tactical Asset Allocation', SSRN 962461 (2009).
15 A. Clare et al., 'The Trend is Our Friend: Risk Parity, Momentum and

good system for investing in equities, most importantly because it avoids heavy investment losses during market crashes.

Faber examines simple trend-following systems for avoiding heavy drawdowns when investing in risky assets like equities. He shows that holding the S&P 500 index when the market is above its own ten-month moving average, and selling and moving to cash when it drops below the moving average, is a good way to improve the annualised return while simultaneously reducing the associated volatility.

Clare et al. find that trend-following in equities, bonds, commodities and real estate is a better method of allocating assets than widely-used asset allocation methods, achieving the higher returns associated with momentum strategies, but with much reduced volatility.

The momentum effect: pure momentum vs trend-following

The third Idle Investor strategy exploits the momentum effect introduced in Chapter 5, i.e. that those shares and share markets that have already gone up, will likely continue to go up in the future. But how does the strategy benefit from this longstanding phenomenon?

There is a wealth of research in the academic literature that highlights the anomalous momentum effect in financial markets – i.e. that trends tend to predict future performance, both up and down. According to this research, trend-following in risk asset markets like equities using a simple long-term moving average system generates better returns than the market *and* at reduced volatility levels. This superior risk-adjusted performance is largely achieved via avoidance of large drawdowns of the type suffered during the bear markets of 2001-03 and 2007-09.

In particular, these simple trend-following strategies are good at capturing the bulk of equity returns while limiting drawdowns, in particular avoiding the bulk of bear markets, which are exactly the characteristics that we are looking for in an investing system.

Trend Following in Global Asset Allocation', SSRN 2126478 (2012).

However, we should note that these trend-following systems are not foolproof: when markets are in a long-term steady uptrend as from 2003 to 2007, then these systems tend to underperform a classic buy-and-hold strategy.

In Figure 35, I demonstrate the results of two simple momentum and trend-following systems as applied to the UK share market over the period 1990-2012. The first system, the three-month momentum strategy, effectively buys and holds the UK share market (on a monthly basis) when the share market's end-month price level is higher than it was three months' prior, but exits any share market exposure when the share market is lower than its three-month-ago level, and moves to cash.

The second system compares the current share market's level to its own six-month average each month, and buys, or holds, UK shares if the end-month level is higher than this average, but sells and switches to, or remains invested in, cash when lower than the six-month average.

As can be seen from Figure 35, the three-month momentum strategy has performed in line with a buy-and-hold strategy from 1990 to 2012, underperforming during strong uptrends (e.g. 1990-2000), but suffering less during bear markets, i.e. when the share market declines by 20% or more (as judged via the maximum drawdown shown in Figure 36).

The six-month moving average strategy has been even more successful, both substantially outperforming buy-and-hold (9.9% CAGR versus 8.0% for buy-and-hold) and also suffering less during bear market periods such as 2007-2009 (dropping less than 13% compared with the 43% fall for the buy-and-hold strategy).

Despite the fact that these two strategies were only invested in equities 62% and 67% of the time respectively, they achieved far better risk-adjusted performance than buy-and-hold, as they avoided the bulk of the damage done by bear markets.

Figure 35: Results showing momentum strategies have worked well

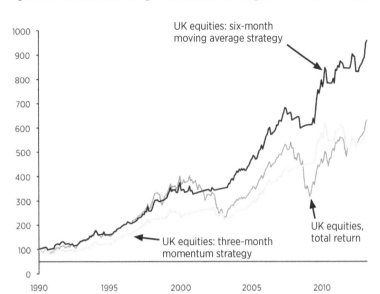

Source: Thomson Reuters Datastream. Note: three-month momentum strategy only invests in equities when share market end-month price level is higher than end closing price three months previous; six-month moving average strategy only invests in equities when the share market index is above its own six-month moving average level.

Figure 36: Momentum strategies carry lower risk than buy-and-hold

	Buy and hold	UK share market positive three-month momentum	UK share market above six-month moving average
Time invested in equities	100%	62%	67%
Total return CAGR	8.00%	7.70%	9.90%
Worst drawdown	-42.90%	-19.20%	-12.70%

Note: three-month momentum and six-month moving average strategies are invested in cash when not invested in equities.

It is all about trend-following, using moving averages

So for our third Idle Investor strategy, we will use a moving average-based trend-following system in order to maximise our returns when the share market is rising, while looking to switch out of shares and into bonds when the share market is instead in a downwards trend.

The key to this mechanical investing system is thus the concept of trend-following. The aim of trend-following is to exploit the fact that the majority of big gains and losses in the share market happen as a result of trends, which we can follow systematically.

It is shocking to realise not only how much damage can be done to your investment by just a limited number of poor weeks, but also how much of a boost is given by the best few weeks of share market performance. This is then the goal of a trend-following system: to capture the bulk of big uptrends in the share market and grow capital effectively during bull markets, but to avoid the bulk of the downtrends and thus preserve capital during bear markets.

CHAPTER 10.

Investing Strategy 3: Multi-Asset Trending Strategy

Using a trend-following method to improve investment returns and reduce risk

The last of the three Idle Investor strategies is the Multi-Asset Trending Strategy. It employs a trend-following investing strategy, using simple moving average-based signals once per month to determine whether to hold higher-risk, higher-return shares via a variety of share ETFs for the following month, or instead to hold a selection of government bond ETFs for the following month. The key investing principle employed here can be neatly encapsulated by the catchphrase: *the trend is your friend.*

You need to be a little more active than in the first two investing strategies, as this involves checking and potentially altering the ETF holdings in your investment portfolio once per month.

Once again, note that by reinvesting all the dividends and interest you receive from the share and bond ETFs each month, you will benefit over time from the compound interest effect.

In this chapter I will discuss the following key building blocks of this strategy:

1. Why the basis of this trend-following strategy is an allocation by geographic region that can result in an asset allocation of 100% shares and 0% bonds at the one extreme, to 0% shares and 100% bonds at the other.

2. The actual returns and risk for the final asset allocation of the strategy.

3. How you can implement this investing strategy, step by step.

4. The pros and cons of this strategy.

5. Finally, there is an action plan at the end of the chapter to summarise all the steps in the investing process for this strategy.

Three steps to long-term outperformance

In the previous chapter, I established that trend-following using moving averages is a good way to maximise investment returns when risky assets are performing well, and to minimise investment losses by switching into lower risk assets when share markets head south.

We can now move on to the three steps that we need to follow to implement our third Idle Investor strategy, the Multi-Asset Trending Strategy (MATS) using ETFs.

Step 1: Divide investment capital into four equal amounts

The first step is to divide your initial investment capital into four equal portions. As an example, let's assume that you start with £10,000 in investment capital, a reasonable amount and less than the current annual shares ISA limit.

This will allow you to invest in four slightly different investment strategies (also sometimes referred to here as *sub-funds*), all of which are variants on the same theme but which together will give us a measure of diversification and thus lower the risk of the overall investment portfolio.

Four pairs of ETFs: equities versus bonds in each case

The four variants on a trend-following theme all involve investing in either a share or bond index ETF at any one time, but in different geographies to add regional diversification – the UK, Europe, the US and emerging markets. This overall portfolio will then always be 100% invested, in a mixture of share and bond ETFs.

The aim here is also to gain exposure in the long-term to the various share market anomalies described in Chapter 5, including the small-cap, value and low volatility effects.

The four sets of equities or bonds pairings that are used in this investing system are:

1. **UK mid-cap equities** versus **UK government bonds**. This pairing is chosen to take advantage of the long-term small-cap premium observed in many academic studies. Example ETFs for these two asset classes are the iShares FTSE 250 ETF (code: MIDD) and the SPDR Barclays 15+ Year Gilt ETF (code: GLTL).

2. **European low volatility equities** versus **European government bonds**. This adds geographic diversification to continental Europe, including to European currencies such as the euro. This pairing also gets exposure to the risk-adjusted outperformance of low volatility shares. Example ETFs are: iShares MSCI Europe Minimum Variance ETF (code: IMV) and iShares Barclays Euro Aggregate Bond ETF (code: IEAG).

3. **US small-cap equities** versus **US government bonds**: This adds further geographic and currency diversification to US assets and also takes exposure to the small-cap premium. Example ETFs: iShares US S&P 600 Small-Cap ETF (code ISP6) and iShares US Aggregate Bond ETF (code: SUAG).

4. **Emerging market equities** versus **emerging market government bonds**: This adds regional diversification, gaining exposure to the higher-growth emerging market countries such as China, India, Brazil, Indonesia and Mexico. Example ETFs: iShares MSCI Emerging Markets Minimum Volatility (code EMV) and iShares Barclays Emerging Market USD Government Bond ETF (code: SEMB).

A summary of the four regional sub-funds is shown in Figure 37.

Figure 37: ETF choices for the four sub-funds

| Area | Share ETF | | Bond ETF | |
	Code	Name	Code	Name
UK	MIDD	iShares FTSE 250 ETF	GLTL	SPDR Barclays 15+ Year Gilt ETF
Europe	IMV	iShares MSCI Europe Min Variance ETF	IEAG	iShares Barclays Euro Aggregate Bond ETF
US	ISP6	iShares US S&P Small-Cap 600 ETF	SUAG	iShares US Aggregate Bond ETF
Emerging markets	EMV	iShares MSCI Emerging Markets Min Volatility ETF	SEMB	iShares Barclays Emerging Market USD Government Bond ETF

Step 2: End-month decision: shares or bonds?

When you first invest your starting investment capital, and then thereafter at the end of each month, you need to allocate the capital in each of the four investment segments either to the relevant share ETF or bond ETF.

How do we do this?

At this point, we introduce our trend-following system.

Trend-following, comparing end-month price level to moving average

For each of the four sub-funds, we are going to compare the end-month price level of a share market index to its own multi-month moving average. My extensive back-tests have shown that the best signals for when to buy and sell share exposure have come from tracking the most popular benchmark indices in each region, as they are most avidly tracked by the financial community and attract the greatest trading volumes. They have thus proved to be the best barometers of market sentiment towards shares in the different regions over time. So the benchmark share market indices we are going to compare at the end of each month to their own multi-month moving averages are:

1. UK: FTSE 100 index

2. Europe: Euro STOXX 50 index

3. Both the US and emerging markets: US S&P 500 index

This is summarised in Figure 38.

Figure 38: Share market indices to use for the four sub-funds

	Sub-fund	Share market indicator	Moving average signal – number of months (days)
1	UK mid-cap equities/UK govt. bonds	FTSE 100	3 (90)
2	Europe low volatility equities/Euro govt. bonds	EuroSTOXX 50	3 (90)
3	US small-cap equities/US govt. bonds	US S&P 500	3 (90)
4	Emerging market equities/EM govt. bonds	US S&P 500	2 (60)

You will also notice that the number of months to use to calculate the moving average is different in one case: while the standard time period for the moving averages is three months, I use only two months for the Emerging Market (EM) sub-fund, given the often higher volatility of both EM equities and bonds versus those in the more developed economies.

If you are using a share price chart system like Yahoo Finance that operates in days rather than months, then I would substitute a 90-day moving average for three months and a 60-day moving average for two months.

Allocating each sub-fund to shares or bonds

For each sub-fund, we test whether the benchmark index used is above its two or three-month moving average (according to the table in Figure 38) at the end of the month. If it is, then we allocate the sub-fund entirely to the equity ETF.

If it rests below the moving average, then the sub-fund is instead allocated 100% to the bond ETF. If you were previously invested in the equity ETF, then this means selling the entire equity ETF and reinvesting 100% of the proceeds into the bond ETF.

In the case of the UK sub-fund, at the end of March 2013 (see Figure 39), the benchmark FTSE 100 index is some distance above its own three-month (90-day) moving average; thus for the month of April, the UK sub-fund would have been invested in the UK FTSE 250 ETF, i.e. in the share fund rather than the bond fund.

This process is repeated for each of the four sub-funds, allocating each sub-fund either entirely to the appropriate equity ETF or to the bond ETF, and if required selling the existing ETF holding and reinvesting the proceeds entirely in the new choice. That is it for the monthly asset reallocation process.

The total return performance generated was 45% over the calendar year, taking the value of the sub-fund up from an initial value of 25 at the end of December 2011 to 36.2 (after trading costs) by the end of 2012.

Figure 39: End-March 2013 – FTSE 100 index signals buy UK shares

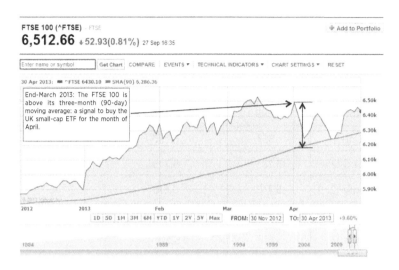

Source: Yahoo Finance.

I have modelled this process over calendar year 2012 for the UK mid-caps/UK government bonds sub-fund in Figure 40.

Here we can see that this sub-fund was invested, on the basis of the end-month FTSE 100 index level versus its three-month moving average, for nine months out of the 12 possible in the UK MID 250 equity ETF, and for three months in the UK government bond ETF.

Figure 40: Month-end reallocation (UK mid-caps, UK bonds)

End of month	FTSE 100 level	FTSE 100 three-month moving average	Difference
Dec-12	6,277	6,014	263
Nov-12	5,898	5,849	49
Oct-12	5867	5,797	70
Sep-12	5,783	5,745	37
Aug-12	5,742	5,616	46
Jul-12	5,712	5,639	72
Jun-12	5,635	5,509	126
May-12	5,571	5,543	28
Apr-12	5,321	5,602	-288
Mar-12	5,738	5,793	-55
Feb-12	5,769	5,774	-5
Jan-12	5,872	5,708	163
Dec-11	5,682	5,586	95

Source: Yahoo Finance.

Reallocation decision		Total return %, next month		Total UK sub-fund value
UK mid-caps	UK govt. bonds	UK mid-caps	UK govt. bonds	
✓		3.10%		36.2
✓		0.60%		35.1
✓		2.30%		34.9
✓		3.60%		34.1
✓		3.90%		32.9
✓		1.90%		31.7
✓		2.80%		31.1
✓			2.90%	30.2
	✓		2.00%	29.4
	✓		-1.60%	28.8
	✓	0.00%		29.3
✓		8.50%		27.1
✓				25

Step 3: End-April, rebalance the four sub-funds to hold the same capital allocation

One key component of portfolio risk reduction, combined with a small element of contrarian value investing, is yearly rebalancing of the four sub-funds, so that none of them get much bigger than the others, thus keeping the investment risk fairly even between the sub-funds over time.

How is this achieved?

Once a year, at the end of April, you also need to perform a rebalancing between the four sub-funds so that they once again hold the same amount of capital. Let us say, for example, that after one year, your investment capital has grown (including dividends) from an initial £10,000 to £11,200, an overall increase of 12% on the year.

However, this increase is an average of the performance of the four sub-funds. In an extreme example, this could be achieved by three of the four sub-funds not growing at all, but the fourth sub-fund enjoying stellar growth of 48%, taking its value from £2,500 at the start of the year to £3,700 at the end of the year.

In this strategy, I reinvest all dividends received, which are typically paid twice per year by the ETFs. The dividends received are then added to the sub-fund in which they are generated, and then reinvested into the ETF held by the sub-fund the next time there is a change in the ETF held (so as to avoid unnecessary trading costs).

Why at the end of April?

I choose this particular time in the year as it represents the point at which typically the seasonal effect in favour of shares diminishes, with May being the first month of the year where one should instead favour the lower risk government bond asset class.

As per the example below (Figure 41), at the end of April in year 1, the rebalancing would involve resetting the capital invested in each of the sub-funds to 25% of the new total portfolio value, which has risen over the year from 100 to 112. Thus each sub-fund should start May of year 1 with 28 invested. In this case, this involves selling 9 from the emerging markets sub-fund, and reinvesting 3 in each of the other sub-funds to bring them all up to 28 capital invested.

Figure 41: Example of yearly rebalancing of the four sub-funds

	UK mid-cap	Europe low volume	US small-cap	Emerging markets	Total
End of April year 0	25	25	25	25	100
Gain over 12 months	0	0	0	50%	
End of April year 1	25	25	25	37	112
Rebalancing moves	3	3	3	-9	
New capital invested	28	28	28	28	112

Historical performance of this system

The following back-test followed the four sub-funds from 1990, making the allocation decision between shares and bonds in each one at the end of the month, and then rebalancing the capital between the four sub-funds at the end of every April. The results are shown in Figure 42.

We can see that the Moving Average Trend-following Strategy (MATS) really started to outperform the UK stock market from the beginning of 1998 and managed to avoid the 2000-03 and 2007-09 bear markets in shares, being invested in bonds over almost the entirety of these two periods.

Figure 42: Strong performance of MATS 1990-2013

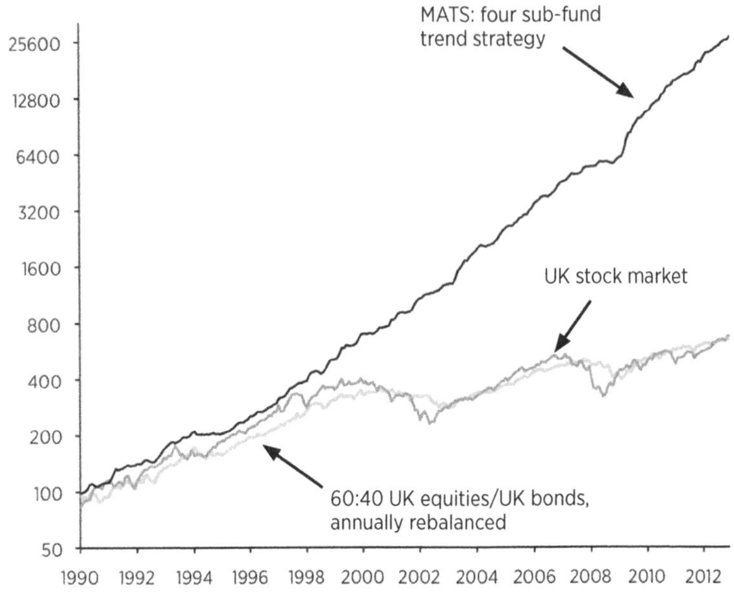

Source: Bloomberg. Note: Logarithmic scale used.

Over the 23-year period from the start of 1990 to the end of 2012, the MATS portfolio would have generated a CAGR of over 27% per annum, with no down years from 1995 onwards. The calendar year performance of MATS each year from 1990 is presented in Figure 43, including trading costs (the costs of buying and selling the equity and bond ETFs) and also dividends and bond coupons that would have been received and reinvested.

Both the benefits of trend-following and the benefits of diversification can be seen: this trend-following strategy switching between shares and bonds has generated positive returns consistently since 1995. Remember that when share markets fall, government bonds tend to post positive returns, particularly when including the bond coupons paid out as interest.

Figure 43: Performance of MATS, year by year

Calendar year	UK mid-caps/UK bonds	EU low volatility/ EU bonds	US small-caps/US bonds	Emerging markets/ EM bonds	MATS: overall strategy
Average	26.10%	25.90%	25.90%	31.60%	27.60%
2012	45.30%	35.70%	30.30%	37.30%	37.00%
2011	20.00%	48.70%	22.10%	17.20%	25.80%
2010	63.60%	21.00%	62.70%	49.10%	48.40%
2009	43.40%	80.20%	68.20%	129.80%	77.20%
2008	35.30%	7.70%	14.60%	-14.40%	9.70%
2007	12.70%	23.10%	28.00%	24.50%	22.00%
2006	26.80%	56.50%	29.40%	35.80%	36.50%
2005	43.30%	17.10%	29.90%	34.30%	31.10%
2004	25.00%	45.30%	30.20%	28.20%	31.70%
2003	52.10%	52.80%	38.50%	52.60%	48.70%
2002	20.60%	16.20%	27.00%	21.30%	21.40%
2001	34.00%	35.20%	29.90%	47.30%	36.40%
2000	15.40%	18.20%	19.80%	-3.70%	11.80%
1999	34.50%	26.20%	28.00%	55.20%	35.90%
1998	48.70%	18.50%	28.80%	29.80%	30.80%
1997	18.20%	28.70%	42.60%	38.10%	31.80%
1996	22.30%	29.10%	17.30%	4.40%	20.50%
1995	6.60%	26.60%	28.90%	-	20.00%
1994	1.30%	-14.30%	10.70%	-	-1.70%
1993	19.00%	56.10%	-1.00%	-	22.50%
1992	26.20%	-0.20%	42.30%	-	21.90%
1991	26.80%	40.70%	6.80%	-	24.10%
1990	15.90%	2.40%	16.80%	-	11.70%

Note: All figures are total return in sterling terms (including dividends/ coupons paid), and include trading costs. Data not available for emerging markets shares and bonds 1990-95.

On top of that, we can see that the best yearly performance varies from year to year between the four sub-funds: the emerging markets shares/bonds sub-fund has posted the best yearly performance four times over the 23-year span, but it also posted the worst yearly performance of the four sub-funds three times.

The UK FTSE 250/UK government bond sub-fund may only have been the best performer five times in 23 years, but this sub-fund was the only one that posted positive yearly performance for 22 out of the 23 years, most notably even during the two share bear markets of the 2000s.

A word on investment risk

As far as investment risk goes, you can see from the data in Figure 43 that the return profile for MATS is relatively smooth – with fairly consistent yearly returns – particularly in comparison to a buy-and-hold equities strategy. Figure 44 displays the monthly volatility of investment returns graphically.

Effectively, the worst falls from peak for the MATS portfolio were seen in 1994, which was the only period during the 23-year span where both equities and government bonds fell at the same time, with MATS suffering an 8%+ drawdown from peak at worst. However, from that point onwards negative monthly returns have been surprisingly limited, demonstrating the effectiveness of this form of trend-following in limiting losses by switching investment exposure into bonds before much investment performance drains away.

Figure 44: Very limited monthly drawdowns for MATS since 1994

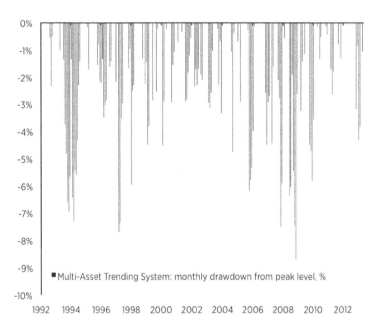

Multi-Asset Trending System: monthly drawdown from peak level, %

Looking forward, performance is unlikely to be as strong

Before getting too excited about the historic performance data presented here, let us not forget that the last couple of decades have benefited from a constant bull market in government bonds, with average returns at least as high as for shares at over 8% per annum on average. But with current bond yields as low as they are (under 3% even for UK 10-year gilts), it is difficult to see how government bonds can achieve returns of this scale going forwards.

That said, when you consider the paucity of investment options facing the average investor today, with both cash interest rates and even government bond yields now so low, I believe that this low volatility investing system is an attractive, low-maintenance alternative.

Outperformance driven partly by share market anomalies, EM currencies

The four sub-funds employed in the MATS system take advantage of various share market anomalies described in Chapter 5 – value, small-cap, momentum and low volatility – plus of course exposure to higher-growth economies and generally appreciating foreign currencies via the emerging markets strategy.

Interestingly, it should be borne in mind that over the last decade or so, some two-thirds of the investment returns in pounds or US dollars have been generated via appreciating emerging market currencies, rather than the underlying local market performance of shares or bonds. Given the near-zero interest rate strategy still being employed currently by central banks in the US, UK, continental Europe and Japan, it is difficult to see this long-term emerging market currency appreciation trend changing.

The Multi-Asset Trending Strategy (MATS)

1. **Trend-following captures upside, limits drawdowns**: MATS compares the current price level of a share market benchmark index (such as the FTSE 100) with its own multi-month moving average in order to determine whether to invest in a higher-risk share ETF or a lower-risk bond ETF.

2. **Investment capital divided equally into four sub-funds**: Take your initial investment capital and split it into four equal amounts. These amounts will be invested in each of four different trend-following share/bond strategies.

3. **End-month choice between a share and bond ETF in each sub-fund**: At the end of each month, for each sub-fund in turn, compare the end-month price level of the given benchmark index with the appropriate moving average of that index. If the end-month price lies above the moving average, then allocate the sub-fund's entire capital to the relevant share ETF (e.g. UK Small-Cap ETF), otherwise allocate the entire capital to the relevant bond ETF (e.g. UK government bond ETF). This may involve selling

the existing ETF holding in the sub-fund to switch the capital into the other ETF option.

4. **End-April yearly rebalancing of capital between sub-funds**: Once per year at the end of April, the capital in each sub-fund needs to be rebalanced so that each sub-fund starts May with the same amount of capital. This may involve selling part of outperforming sub-funds and reinvesting in underperforming sub-funds.

5. **Historic back-test performance strong**: Historic performance of MATS has been strong, averaging double-digit returns since 1995.

6. **Unlikely to be as strong in future, given current bond yields**: However, this historic performance has benefited from a long-term bull market in government bonds. With yields now close to 50+ year lows, this level of bond market returns is unlikely to be sustainable in future, with far lower expected returns. However, the trend-following strategy should still deliver consistent returns with relatively low associated investment risk.

Action Plan: Strategy 3 –The Multi-Asset Trending Strategy (MATS)

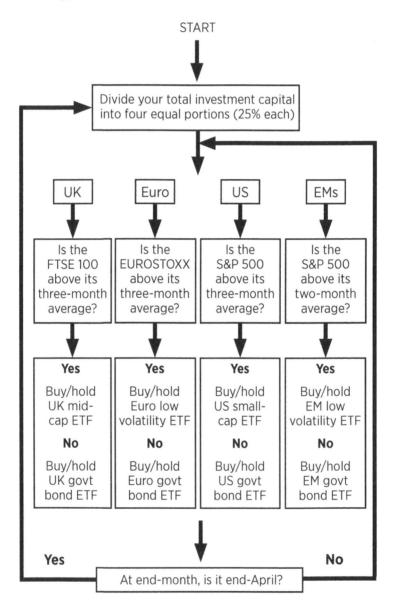

START

Divide your total investment capital into four equal portions (25% each)

UK	Euro	US	EMs
Is the FTSE 100 above its three-month average?	Is the EUROSTOXX above its three-month average?	Is the S&P 500 above its three-month average?	Is the S&P 500 above its two-month average?
Yes Buy/hold UK mid-cap ETF	**Yes** Buy/hold Euro low volatility ETF	**Yes** Buy/hold US small-cap ETF	**Yes** Buy/hold EM low volatility ETF
No Buy/hold UK govt bond ETF	**No** Buy/hold Euro govt bond ETF	**No** Buy/hold US govt bond ETF	**No** Buy/hold EM govt bond ETF

Yes   **No**

At end-month, is it end-April?

Summary

Asset allocation	1. Four share ETFs: UK mid-caps; US small-caps; European low volatility; emerging markets low volatility. 2. Four government bond ETFs: UK gilts; US treasuries; Eurozone government bonds; emerging markets sovereign bonds.
Idleness indicator (frequency of action required)	1. Monthly, i.e. 12 times per year – at the beginning of each month decide for each of the four regions whether to hold a share or a bond ETF. 2. Yearly rebalancing of the four regions at end-April so that at that point, the investment amount allocated to each of the four regions is equal. Remember at the beginning of each month to reinvest any dividends you have received over the previous month in the four ETFs chosen by the strategy.
Investing principles	1. Diversify over time by holding shares when they are in an uptrend, otherwise by holding bonds. 2. Invest in shares for long-term growth. 3. Invest in bonds for income and lower risk.
Investing strategy	Trend-following: For each of four geographic regions (UK, Europe, US, emerging markets), hold a share ETF if the moving average-based stock market signal for that region is positive, or else hold a bond ETF.
Asset split (can change each month)	From 100% equities, 0% bonds to 0% equities, 100% bonds
Long-term performance (compound annual growth rate)	27.6% CAGR (1990-2012)
Risk (worst fall peak-to-trough)	2007-2009: -9%

CHAPTER 11.

Six Key Investment Trends For the Future

I will now look at some key investment trends that long-term investors should be aware of.

Below I list six trends that have been in place for some time, but which look likely to remain very important for investors to consider for the next few years:

1. Inflation to remain subdued for a long time, so cash rates will remain very low.

2. Future bond returns will be lower given the depressed levels of current bond yields.

3. Encouragement from the UK government to save more via ISAs, employee pensions, personal pensions. And pension flexibility to boost investment in income shares.

4. The rising risk that property investments, such as buy-to-let, will be taxed more heavily as the government tries to pay off the national debt.

5. The *hunt for yield* will underline how important reinvested dividends are in driving total return from shares.

6. Exchange-traded funds (ETFs) will continue to broaden their appeal to the retail investor and become a much more commonplace way for people to invest their savings.

I will now go into some more detail on each of these six trends and the impact they will have on investors.

1. Interest rates on cash savings to remain depressed

Thanks to the long-lasting aftermath of the 2008 financial crisis, interest rates on UK savings accounts at banks and building societies remain mired at historic lows. While this is great news for mortgage borrowers who see the benefits of these ultra-low interest rates in lower monthly mortgage payments, it is painful for savers who can now only achieve around 1.4% at best on an instant-access savings account.

This is a far cry from the situation during 1960-2008, when such accounts offered an average annual interest rate of 6.2% (Figure 45).

Figure 45: UK average savings rates, 1960-2015

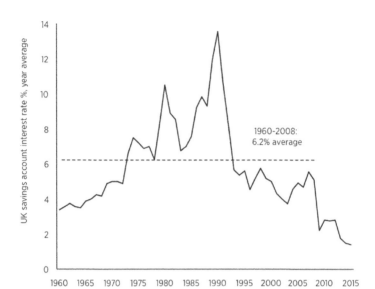

Source: www.swanlowpark.co.uk.

In general, interest rates on cash deposits and mortgages are tied to the Bank of England's Base Rate, which itself is determined by the Bank's policy of inflation targeting (the Bank aims to keep UK inflation close to its 2% target over time).

However, as Figure 46 illustrates, the Bank of England did not manage to prevent UK inflation (measured by the yearly change in the consumer price index – CPI) from falling well below this 2% target level in 2014, with the headline CPI inflation rate dropping to only 0.5% as of December 2014 and core CPI (excluding the more volatile food and energy components) not far from the 1% mark.

Figure 46: UK inflation remains well below the Bank of England's target

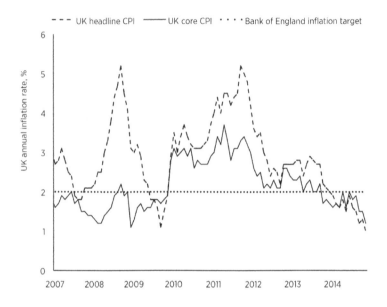

Source: Bank of England.

Bottom line

The UK's interest rates will remain ultra-low for years to come, as the UK struggles with the lack of inflation. Savers will have to look elsewhere for decent investment returns, as the pre-2008 average of a 6.2% savings account rate will remain but a dim and distant memory.

2. Bonds will not give as good an investment return as over the last few decades

Over the last 15 years or so, ten-year UK government bond (gilt) yields have averaged 4%. Indeed, gilt yields actually averaged between 4% and 5% consistently between 1999 and 2008 (Figure 47).

Figure 47: UK gilt yields are at historic lows

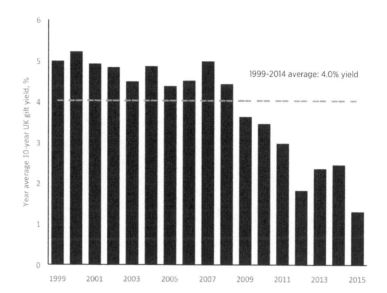

Source: FTSE.

Fast forward to early 2015 and an investor in UK gilts is presented with a far less attractive proposition, with a ten-year UK gilt offering a yield today of only 1.3%.

This is very important for long-term investors, as history tells us that the vast bulk of the total return (price gain plus interest payments, reinvested over time) in UK gilts has come from the income element, i.e. the regular coupon payments, rather than gains in bond prices.

Since 1999, the FTSE UK Gilt index has delivered a CAGR of 5.5% including reinvested income, while the price index alone has only generated a 0.3% CAGR over the last 15 years (see Figure 48). The 5.2% difference is the effect of that reinvested income.

But of course, with only a 1.3% yield available to those investing in UK gilts today, the compounded effect of this income reinvested over time will not be anything like as significant as has historically been the case.

Figure 48: The bulk of historic bonds investment returns came from income

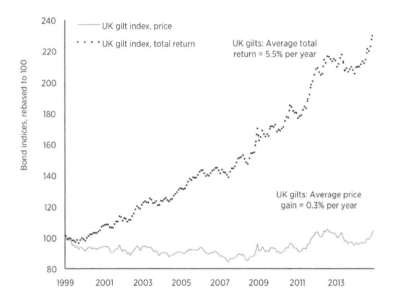

Source: FTSE.

Bottom line

Investors will have to get used to far lower future returns from bonds than we have been used to in the past, with average returns of 1% to 2% per year more likely in future.

3. The UK government will encourage us to save more

The logical consequence of these lower investment returns from safe assets like cash and government bonds is that we will need to save more of our income, to make up for these lower expected investment returns.

The government has already gone a long way in trying to tempt us with savings carrots such as increasing the amount of money we can salt away free of capital gains or income tax in individual savings accounts (ISAs), with adults now able to save up to £15,240 per tax year (as of the tax year 2015/2016) in an ISA in any number of assets from cash to shares.

The government has also tried to make personal pensions more attractive by increasing the freedom and choice in pensions. The new *pension freedom* rules have made saving in a pension even more attractive in a number of ways, but this is a complex subject which I don't have the space to go into here in any detail.

Suffice it to say that the government will continue to encourage us to save more in a number of tax-efficient vehicles for our old age, which will put the onus more and more on us to become more active investors whether we like it or not.

Bottom line

Using a low-maintenance ETF-based investment strategy, such as one of the three Idle Investor strategies, will become more and more important for those looking to have a decent level of retirement income to enjoy.

4. There is a big risk that direct property investments become less attractive

However, where the government giveth, the government can also taketh away. While they will continue to encourage long-term and retirement saving, we should not forget that Her Majesty's Treasury also has an enormous pile of national debt to pay off over time – over £1.4 trillion as of August 2014.

But what is £1.4 trillion? A very big number, for sure. Put another way, it is £1.4 thousand thousand million, or 77% of the value of the entire UK economy! In order to chip away at this colossal amount of debt, the government will clearly need to (a) cut spending, and (b) raise revenues.

Cuts to public spending are well under way already and likely to get more severe in the future. However, what is more important to investors is that the government will likely also look to raise more revenue via taxes.

Where might they look to raise this extra revenue?

I would suggest that one obvious avenue is via higher property taxes, as property has the distinction of being relatively easy to tax as it is immobile, unlike individuals or companies who can relocate abroad for tax reasons.

According to the mortgage company Paragon, at the end of 2014 some 18% of homes in the UK were owned by private landlords, which is 4.9 million homes in total. This is double the 2.5 million homes in private landlords' hands back in 2002, a high rate of growth over the intervening 12 years. What is more, according to the government's own estimates, this growth trend in buy-to-let property investment is likely to result in over one-in-three homes being owned by private landlords by 2032.

Very low cash savings rates and falling mortgage borrowing costs have been a prime driver behind this explosive growth in the private rented sector; but it also provides a wonderful opportunity for both local and central governments to raise revenue, at a time when it is desperately needed.

Bottom line

The relative attractions of buy-to-let property investment are likely to become progressively less alluring over time as the government looks to property to raise tax revenue. Alternatives like the Idle Investor strategies will become more appealing in large part for tax reasons when used within an ISA or self-invested personal pension (SIPP).

5. The hunt for yield will drive investors towards dividend growth shares

Given the historically low interest rates on offer from cash deposit accounts and government bonds, where will income-starved investors look to generate yields on their long-term savings?

Judging by Figure 49, the answer seems ever more likely to be shares, given the historically high yield spread of some 2.7% between the FTSE 100 index dividend yield (4.0%) and the yield on ten-year UK gilts (1.3%). Prior to the 2008 financial crisis, UK share dividend yields had been consistently *lower* than gilt yields for 50 years since the 1950s!

Figure 49: UK shares offer by far the best yields today

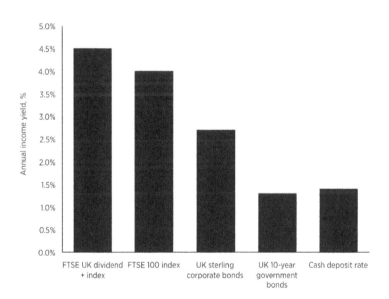

Source: FTSE, Bloomberg. Note: Yields correct as of end-January, 2015.

This is one reason for favouring investment in high dividend and dividend-growth shares, represented by the FTSE UK Dividend+ index in the figure above, offering a 4.5% dividend yield, which is some 0.5% better than the FTSE 100 index and some 1.8% better than even UK corporate bonds (which yield 2.7% on average).

Over the six years since the share markets began to recover in 2009, the UK Dividend+ index has delivered a cumulative total return (price gain plus dividends reinvested) of +136%, compared with only +90% for the FTSE 100 index over the same period. (See Figure 50.)

Figure 50: The UK dividend index has beaten the FTSE 100 by 4% per year since 2009

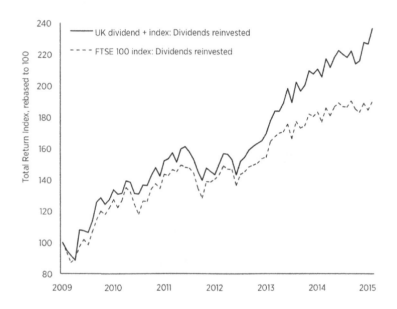

Source: FTSE.

Bottom line

I expect these higher dividend and dividend growth-focused shares to be in high demand from income-seeking investors given the diminishing attractions of bonds, which should drive further outperformance from this group of shares similar to that seen from 2009 to date.

6. Exchange-traded funds to become much more mainstream investment vehicles

On the face of it, Europe-listed exchange-traded funds (ETFs) have seen great success over the past few years, with net inflows totalling over $61 billion for the calendar year 2014, and total assets under management swelling to $467 billion, according to industry leader BlackRock. This makes Europe as a whole the second largest global market for ETFs after the US.

However, despite thousands of ETFs being available in the UK and continental Europe, they are still relatively little-known and little-used by retail investors. An estimated 85% of all ETFs bought in Europe are bought by institutional investors and only 15% by retail investors; in the US where the use of ETFs for investment is better-established, fully 50% of ETF volumes are accounted for by retail investors.

The low costs, transparency and ease of buying and selling like a share (but without stamp duty to pay) are all key attractions for ETFs, versus investment in unit trusts or individual shares. However, up to now it seems that ETFs are simply not well known or understood by the majority of the UK and European investing public.

I think that this is in the process of changing. In the US, for example, we can see that ETFs are largely replacing US mutual funds (like UK unit trusts) in certain core fund categories such as US Equity. This is hardly surprising given that many ETFs now charge an annual management fee of well under 0.1% to compare to the 1%+ that is usually charged by a mutual fund/unit trust in the US or UK (and often more in continental Europe).

While ETFs are still not yet considered as a viable investment option by the majority of retail investors in Europe, significant recent regulatory changes, such as the UK's Regulatory Distribution Review (RDR), have increased scrutiny over the fees that investment funds like unit trusts charge.

This should boost the use of low-cost ETFs, aided by big investor education programmes launched by the largest European ETF providers such as iShares (owned by BlackRock) and x-Trackers (owned by Deutsche Bank).

Bottom-line

ETFs are poised to enter the mainstream of retail investing in the UK and continental Europe, which should only serve to lower costs further, increase liquidity and also increase the choice of ETFs via the expansion of the so-called *smart beta* ETF universe – these are ETFs which use specific quantitative strategies designed to deliver outperformance against the main benchmark indices such as the FTSE 100.

This trend should magnify the attractions of ETFs to long-term investors. Of course, the Idle Investor strategies are an excellent way to profit from this trend!

How will the three Idle Investor strategies cope with these trends?

I should say that I had these long-term investment trends in mind when I was designing the three Idle Investor strategies – so, naturally, they should all cope well with these six trends.

Each of the three strategies will cope with the lower expected returns for investors from cash deposits, and also from long-term bond investments, by helping investors to take exposure to the higher expected long-term investment returns from shares, while limiting the investment risk taken in several ways.

This was quite evident from the substantial outperformance of each of the three Idle Investor strategies over the course of 2014, at a time when the UK stock market delivered an essentially flat calendar year performance.

I would however caution that the lower expected investment returns from bonds and cash will inevitably mean that the three strategies are unlikely to deliver the returns that have been demonstrated in the various back-tests over the past couple of decades. Remember that over this period of time both cash interest rates and bond yields were far higher than they are today, thus delivering higher overall returns for each of the strategies.

Nevertheless, I believe that a consistent application of any one of the three investing strategies described in this book will deliver superior returns over the long term to the patient investor; well above what he or she could achieve by investing on a buy-and-hold basis in shares and/or bonds, not to mention cash.

Variations on a theme: possible improvements to the three strategies

Clearly there are always a number of variations that can be applied to any one of these three strategies. However, I have not described any variations here in order to keep this book as short and simple to understand as possible.

But I would say that one key variation that some may like to consider would be the use of dividend-focused share ETFs like the iShares UK Dividend+ ETF instead of the UK mid-cap components of the three strategies, in order to boost the income delivered to the investor.

And, of course, with more ETFs being introduced to the market all the time, there could well be even more attractive ETFs to use for the share or bond components of each of the three strategies.

CHAPTER 12.

Idle Investor Maxims

Finally, to wrap the book up, I list below 18 key principles for Idle Investors.

1. **Buyer beware**. Financial experts do not always have your best interests at heart.

2. **Knowledge alone is not enough**. Successful investing is certainly not just about having the necessary financial knowledge; there is much more to it than retaining facts and figures.

3. **Patience and inaction**. These are vastly underrated investment behaviours.

4. **Fund managers underperform**. The majority of active fund managers underperform equity indices over an extended period of time.

5. **Fund managers are generally not worth it**. Fund managers are on average not worth the additional fees they charge over and above an equivalent index-tracking fund.

6. **Passive investing is cheaper**. Beware the insidious effects of initial and annual charges and other costs on net long-term investment performance when choosing funds. Index funds and

ETFs are usually a better vehicle than actively-managed funds given their lower cost structure.

7. **The Buffett Myth**. The fact that a select few super-investors have outperformed the share markets in the long term does not prove that most, or even many, active fund managers can do the same.

8. **Don't screen watch**. By all means be interested in or even passionate about investment and investment-related topics, but do not obsessively watch market indices or the daily fluctuations in price of your own investments. That way madness (or at least underperformance of your investments) lies.

9. **Saving money is as important as making it**. Do not underestimate the role of volatility in undermining an investor's compound returns over time. An investment with low volatility in its investment returns will typically give superior profits over time to one which sees returns swing from positive to negative and back again.

10. **Know your own risk comfort level**. Knowing your own capacity for loss is an important first step in determining your ultimate investment strategy for your savings. But you need to be honest with yourself, as you will be kidding no one but yourself ultimately.

11. **Avoid the fast buck mentality**. You must not take so much risk that you endanger your ability to sleep soundly at night! Better to accept a lower level of risk and a lower expected investment return, than to attempt to make a fast buck. More often than not this expectation is unrealistic and often leads to painful losses. Remember, the tortoise won the race, not the hare.

12. **Don't keep all your cash eggs in one basket**. Limit your cash deposits to £85,000 per person per bank/building society. Think about putting cash in the names of your partners and children in order that your cash savings benefit to the maximum from the Financial Services Compensation Scheme's £85,000 insurance coverage.

13. **Diversify asset classes**. Asset class diversification via multi-asset portfolios can offer better returns and a lower investment risk profile compared with single asset classes. But only up to a point:

over-diversify and you will achieve a lower investment return without a corresponding further reduction in investment risk.

14. **Longer holding period = lower risk of loss**. The risk of loss over a given period in a risky asset class like equities declines quickly as the holding period is extended. So only think of investing in risky assets if you can leave the capital invested for at least five years, preferably even longer.

15. **Preserve capital**. Preservation of investment capital when risk markets decline is just as important, if not more important, than chasing returns in risky asset classes when conditions are propitious.

16. **Beware of debt**. Debt is a financial weapon of mass destruction – handle with extreme care! Remember, financial gearing magnifies both gains and losses.

17. **Near-zero interest rates to persist**. Central banks (e.g. the Bank of England) are very likely to continue to favour supporting economic growth over curbing near-term inflation, thus keeping interest rates far lower than in a normal economic cycle.

18. **Use tax-efficient investments**. Tax-advantaged investment vehicles like ISAs and private pensions can be a very efficient way to invest capital for the long term. But they are subject to a number of potential drawbacks such as (a) accessibility to the capital in an emergency, (b) the fees and charges levied on the tax-advantaged fund structure, and (c) the risk of changes in government regulation that could diminish the tax-based attractiveness of these products.

It leaves me just to wish you the best of luck in your investing endeavours. I hope that these three Idle Investor strategies will stand you in good stead for the investing road ahead.

.

Useful sources of financial information

I provide below a list of resources for investing – primarily on the internet – that I've found useful. The following is divided into 13 sections:

1. General investing
2. Financial education
3. Online stockbrokers for buying ETFs, other funds and shares
4. Financial news and market prices
5. Macro-economic and investment themes
6. Interesting investment blogs
7. Financial data
8. Financial history and economic observations
9. Index providers
10. ETF providers
11. UK investment funds
12. Multimedia material on financial history and investment themes
13. Useful books on investment

1. General investing

Money Observer

www.moneyobserver.com

As well as a number of financial news articles and features, there are also videos on different investment topics such as retail bond investing.

MoneySavingExpert.com

www.moneysavingexpert.com/savings

Useful guides to the best ISAs, savings accounts, annuities and pensions.

Moneywise

www.moneywise.co.uk/investing

A straightforward website that has a number of simple-to-read articles for first-time investors.

The Motley Fool (UK)

www.fool.co.uk

A good source of UK share-specific investing ideas and analysis. There is also a good section on investing basics.

This is Money

www.thisismoney.co.uk/money

The financial website for the *Daily Mail*, hosting articles on saving and investing, as well as other personal finance topics.

Which?

www.which.co.uk

The Which? website has a good section on understanding investment risk written in plain English, along with a whole section on savings and investments.

Yahooo Finance

uk.finance.yahoo.com

A good resource for market and share prices, storing a virtual portfolio, reading market news and drawing share or index charts.

2. Financial education

AAII

www.aaii.com

The American Association of Individual Investors has a whole ream of unbiased investor education material available on this website, including how to use inflation-protected bonds in your portfolio.

Investopedia

www.investopedia.com

A great resource for looking up investment terms that you don't understand, with a good section on investing basics.

The Money Advice Service

www.moneyadviceservice.org.uk

An independent service set up by government to help people make the most of their money, giving free, unbiased money advice to everyone across the UK.

unbiased.co.uk

www.unbiased.co.uk

While the primary aim of this website is to put investors in touch with Independent Financial Advisers, there are also a number of very useful finance and investment topics addressed including pensions and retirement, savings and investments, and financial planning.

Valuation guru Professor Aswath Damodaran

pages.stern.nyu.edu/~adamodar

For those looking to understand financial valuation techniques in great detail, Prof. Damodaran has been generous enough to post all his teaching material and writings on this website.

3. Online brokers for ETFs, other funds and shares

Barclays Stockbrokers

www.barclaysstockbrokers.co.uk

A popular online stockbroker for UK investors.

Hargreaves Lansdown

www.hl.co.uk

HL's Knowledge Centre (funds, shares, ISAs, SIPPs) provides a lot of information about investments and pensions, together with a number of free expert guides on subjects such as equity income and ISAs.

TD Direct Investing

www.tddirectinvesting.co.uk

TD Direct is a leading player in online share dealing, ISAs, self-invested pension plans and buying/selling funds. Their website has a number of useful articles in their Guide to Investing.

4. Financial news and market prices

Barrons

online.barrons.com

The website of the Dow Jones-owned weekly investing newspaper is US-oriented for the most part but does contain some European content and a few interesting topics.

Bloomberg

www.bloomberg.com/markets

A good source of market news stories from one of the key market data and news providers to investment banks and financial market professionals. While the website is somewhat US-centric, there are also tabs to access UK- and Europe-specific news.

Breakingviews

blogs.reuters.com/breakingviews

This is particularly useful for those looking for more in-depth but pithy analysis of certain financial news stories.

Digital Look

www.digitallook.com

Digital Look has a range of market news, share charts, company fundamentals data and a portfolio tracking facility all offered free to the retail investor. It also has a handy tool for ranking price performance of shares in different share markets.

Financial Times

www.ft.com

Free access to the UK's premier financial newspaper's articles is severely limited, but still worth using upon registration. The blogs are also interesting to read.

Google Finance

www.google.co.uk/finance

A quick way to browse market news from a variety of online financial news sources (as with Google News), also a way to check share prices or basic fundamental information on a company.

MarketWatch

www.marketwatch.com

Part of the News International/Dow Jones stable together with the *Wall Street Journal* and Barrons. Good for financial market news.

Wall St. Journal Europe

europe.wsj.com

The European version of the WSJ is good for news and analysis, together with its sister website marketwatch.com.

5. Macro-economic and investment themes

Barclays Wealth Behavioural Finance

www.investmentphilosophy.net

Good set of educational videos and tools on the subject of behavioural finance.

Barclays Wealth Compass

www.barclayswealth.com/compass.htm

Barclays Wealth (wealth manager) provides free access to Compass, their monthly investment strategy publication.

Berkshire Hathaway annual letters

www.berkshirehathaway.com/letters/letters.html

The quoted US investment fund of legendary investor Warren Buffett provides free access to the annual letter to Berkshire Hathaway shareholders describing the performance of the fund and investments made, written by Warren Buffett and Charlie Munger. This archive goes back as far as 1977.

Credit Suisse Research Institute

www.credit-suisse.com

This Institute gives free access to a number of reports such as their Global Wealth report.

The Economist

www.economist.com

What to say about this magazine-that-is-not-a-magazine-but-rather-a-newspaper (according to *The Economist*)? Free access to a number of articles, plus a number of blogs.

GMO

www.gmo.com

This Boston-based asset management firm gives online access to their Insights research reports and also their quarterly letter, written by Jeremy Grantham.

The Graham Investor

www.grahaminvestor.com

A useful resource focused on value investing in the style of Benjamin Graham, with articles and share screeners (US-based) aimed at buying shares that trade at a discount to their net current asset value.

International Monetary Fund

www.imf.org/external/pubs/ft/weo/2012/02/index.htm

Their World Economic Outlook publication gives global economic data on regions and countries, including five-year forecasts.

McKinsey Global Institute

www.mckinsey.com/insights

The research branch of this management consultancy firm give free access to a number of their reports on key long-term themes. For example, the rise of the consuming class with increasing urbanisation, and the potential for lithium-ion battery prices to fall dramatically by 2020, potentially boosting demand for electric vehicles.

MoneyWeek

www.moneyweek.com

The website of this popular UK finance magazine has a useful section on economic indicators such as house prices, inflation and the gold price.

OECD

www.oecd.org

A wide-range of topics on the global economy from this supranational research organisation, including a huge database of downloadable economic statistics.

PIMCO

europe.pimco.com

The largest bond fund manager in the world (based on the US west coast) gives regular insights into key global macro-economic themes, asset allocation and their own monthly investment outlook.

QFinance

www.financepractitioner.com

Home to viewpoint articles, explanations of a number of concepts and terms, and hosts a number of blogs to boot.

Seeking Alpha

seekingalpha.com

US-oriented but still useful for ideas on investment themes, macroeconomic trends and ETF selection.

6. Interesting investment blogs

Abnormal Returns

abnormalreturns.com

Tadas Viskanta posts daily a great collection of the best financial market-related web links, featuring interesting articles from all over the internet.

Bank Credit Analyst Research

blog.bcaresearch.com

Excellent global macro-oriented research from this Canadian-based firm. The research itself is aimed at institutional clients like banks and asset managers and is expensive to subscribe to, but this blog gives some free, illuminating insights in a short format.

Barel Karsan

www.barelkarsan.com

This blog largely discusses US value share ideas, but its summaries of classic books on finance and investing are also useful.

Eurosharelab Blog

www.eurosharelab.com/blog

European value investment advice.

Expecting Value

expectingvalue.com

Focused on writing about UK value shares.

Interactive Investor Blogs

www.iii.co.uk/news-opinion/blogs

Interactive Investor hosts three investment bloggers Share Sleuth, The Colonel and Peter Temple, each of which write about UK share and ETF investments.

InvestorTrader

www.investortrader.co.uk

Discussion of investment philosophy and UK share picks.

Monevator

monevator.com

A guide to passive investing in the UK.

Pragmatic Capitalism

pragcap.com

In-depth commentary on various investment themes from Cullen Roche.

The Big Picture

www.ritholtz.com/blog

Barry Ritholtz is a thought-provoking US-based financial blogger who gives his own investment insights, and also provides links to financial articles he finds interesting.

Thoughts from the Frontline

www.frontlinethoughts.com

John Mauldin writes a thought-provoking weekly free newsletter here.

Value-Investing.eu

www.value-investing.eu/blog

As it says, focused on value investing in Europe.

Value Restoration Project

www.valuerestorationproject.com

Another good value investing blog, focused on the US share market principally.

Meb Faber Research

www.mebanefaber.com

Mebane Faber provides a wealth of links and ideas relating to quantitative investing, e.g. on asset allocation.

7. Financial data

Livec Charts

www.livecharts.co.uk

Free charts for indices, shares, commodities and FX.

Ycharts

ycharts.com

A good website for charting UK and global economic data quickly and easily.

Trading Economics

www.tradingeconomics.com

Economic indicators in table and chart form for 196 countries.

Guardian Datablog

www.guardian.co.uk/data

A surprising array of data can be found on this sub-site of the *Guardian's* website, such as the UK's interest rate back to 1694, key charts for understanding the Eurozone's debt crisis and UK inflation versus wages since 1948.

Swanlowpark

swanlowpark.co.uk

An historical comparison of price-inflation, share-market index-tracker funds and savings-accounts in the UK back as far as 1960 in the case of savings rates. The data series can also be downloaded.

Measuring Worth

www.measuringworth.com/ukcompare

Data and calculators for long-term currency, share market and economic growth rates. For example, contains yearly data series for UK inflation and annual average earnings back to 1209, and the London market price of gold from 1718.

Professor Robert Shiller

www.econ.yale.edu/~shiller

US share market data used in Prof. Shiller's book *Irrational Exuberance* can be downloaded from his website, with monthly US share market and macro-economic data series back to 1871.

Wren Investment Advisors

www.wrenadvisers.com.au

Historic financial market data from this Australian investment adviser, including yearly gold prices from 1800, Australian equities from 1875 and the Japanese Nikkei 225 index since 1950.

8. Financial history and economic observations

Federal Reserve Bank of St. Louis, US

timeline.stlouisfed.org

'The Financial Crisis: A Timeline of Events and Policy Actions'

European debt crisis timeline

finance.yahoo.com/news/timeline-evolution-european-debt-crisis-070133430.html

'Timeline: Evolution of the European debt crisis', by Sheila Steiner of Bankrate.com

Tim Harford, the undercover economist

timharford.com

The author of the book *The Undercover Economist* and presenter of the BBC Radio 4 series *More or Less* also writes a blog on a wide variety of economic topics.

Freakonomics

www.freakonomics.com

A blog written by Steven Levitt and Stephen Dubner, the co-authors of the well-received books *Freakonomics* and *Super-Freakonomics*, which were also turned into a 2010 film of the same name. Answers all manner of economics-related questions in a clear fashion. Also a podcast (on iTunes, or www.freakonomics.com/radio/freakonomics-radio-podcast-archive).

Credit Suisse Investment Returns Yearbook(s)

www.credit-suisse.com/uk/en/news-and-expertise/research/credit-suisse-research-institute/publications.html

Co-written by Elroy Dimson, Paul Marsh and Mike Staunton, three academics at London Business School, this report contains lots of very long-term data on economies and markets, such as UK inflation back to 1265!

Barclays Equity Gilt Study

wealth.barclays.com/en_gb/smartinvestor/better-investor/investing-lessons-from-114-years-of-data.html

Another similar study of long-term investment returns from UK equities, bonds and cash.

9. Index providers

S&P Dow Jones Indices

www.spdji.com

This newly merged company controls the two major benchmark blue-chip equity indices in the United States, the Dow Jones Industrial and the Standard & Poor's 500 (S&P). They also offer a number of interesting European dividend-related indices for income and income growth investors such as the S&P European Dividend Aristocrats.

STOXX

www.stoxx.com

This company controls the STOXX series of equity indices in Europe including the EuroSTOXX 50 Euro-wide benchmark index, which is the most liquid pan-European equity index.

FTSE

www.ftse.com

The provider of the UK's benchmark FTSE 100 index, and other UK indices. Also has a global index series.

MSCI

www.msci.com

The controller of the MSCI World equity index, they provide historical international equity benchmark indices in particular for US fund managers.

10. ETF providers

iShares

uk.ishares.com

The biggest provider in the world of exchange-traded funds, covering a multitude of asset classes, regions and strategies. Interesting for their US high-yield credit ETF, the largest of its type. Owned by global fund manager behemoth BlackRock.

Lyxor

www.lyxoretf.co.uk

After iShares, the next biggest ETF provider by market share in Europe is Lyxor. They offer some interesting ETFs such as an expected dividends ETF and a number of commodity ETFs. Owned by French bank Société Générale.

db X-trackers

www.etf.db.com

A wide range of ETFs, including a multi-asset ETF with exposure to equities, bonds and cash. Owned by Deutsche Bank.

ETF Securities

www.etfsecurities.com

The broadest and most comprehensive range of commodity and currency-based ETFs, with ETFs for physical gold bullion, agricultural commodities, energy and a variety of currency ETFs (e.g. US dollar, Euro, Swiss Franc, Australian dollar, Canadian dollar, Swedish Krona, Norwegian Krona).

State Street (SPDR)

www.spdrseurope.com

One of the biggest US ETF providers, it also has some interesting strategies on offer in Europe such as the UK and Europe Dividend Aristocrats ETFs (only investing in the highest-yielding companies that have increased their dividends every year for the past ten years).

Ossiam

www.ossiam.com

Offers equity ETFs based not on market capitalisation but rather on an equal-weighted or minimum variance weighting strategy, both of which generally experience lower volatility than ETFs based on traditional market-cap weighted indices. Affiliate of the French bank Natixis.

11. UK investment funds

Association of Investment Companies

www.theaic.co.uk

The umbrella organisation for UK investment trusts, that are closed-end listed investment funds, typically much cheaper than their unit trust counterparts. Detailed statistics on UK investment trusts can be found on their statistics website, www.aicstats.co.uk.

FE Trustnet

www.trustnet.com

An excellent resource for comparing different unit and investment trusts, and for looking at details of the various funds, including ETFs, pension funds and life insurance products. There is also a good section with education guides which explains a number of key concepts relating to investment funds.

The Investment Association

www.investmentfunds.org.uk

The umbrella organisation for UK unit trusts, including monthly fund flow statistics for tracking the movement of investors' money in and out of the industry as a whole, and for tracking which unit trust sectors are particularly popular or unpopular each month.

Morningstar UK

www.morningstar.co.uk

Provides ratings for investment funds and also now hosts the HemScott fundamental share database.

12. Multimedia material on financial history and investment themes

Business TV

Bloomberg TV

www.bloomberg.com/tv/europe

Live internet feed of the Bloomberg TV channel in Europe, plus a wide selection of video clips on a variety of current economic and market news topics.

CNBC Europe

www.cnbc.com

The website of this business TV channel hosts a large number of short videos of company management and finance markets professionals culled from their live broadcasts.

Reuters TV

uk.reuters.com/video

A collection of video clips from a number of shows including Investing 201, Breakingviews and Fast Forward.

Podcasts

The following podcasts can be found on iTunes, or at the addresses given.

The Motley Fool Moneytalk

www.fool.co.uk/money-talk

A UK-based investment podcast centred mostly on how to select shares to buy.

Loz and Belly

loznbelly.blogspot.fr

The weekly global macro-based investment podcast from GLC's Lawrence Staden and Steven Bell.

Films

Inside Job (2010)

www.imdb.com/title/tt1645089

A 120-minute documentary taking a closer look at what brought about the US financial meltdown, written and directed by Charles Ferguson and starring Matt Damon.

Enron: The Smartest Guys in the Room (2005)

www.imdb.com/title/tt1016268

A 110-minute documentary examining Enron Corporation, which collapsed from being the seventh-largest US company by market capitalisation to bankruptcy in less than one year due to corrupt business practices. Written and directed by Alex Gibney.

13. Useful books on investment

Christopher Browne, *The Little Book of Value Investing* (John Wiley & Sons, 2006)

Warren Buffett, *The Essays of Warren Buffett: Lessons for Corporate America*, Second Edition (Carolina Academic Press, 2012)

David Dreman, *Contrarian Investment Strategies – The Next Generation* (Simon & Schuster, 1999)

Philip Fisher, *Common Stocks and Uncommon Profits and Other Writings* (John Wiley & Sons, 1996)

John Kenneth Galbraith, *The Great Crash 1929* (Penguin, 2009)

Benjamin Graham, *The Intelligent Investor*, revised edition (Collins Business Essentials, 2003)

Joel Greenblatt, *The Little Book That Still Beats the Market: Your Safe Haven in Good Times or Bad* (John Wiley & Sons, 2010)

Daniel Kahneman, *Thinking, Fast and Slow* (Allen Lane, 2011)

Costas Lapavitsas, *Crisis in the Eurozone* (Verso, 2012)

Janet Lowe, *Value Investing Made Easy: Benjamin Graham's Classic Investment Strategy Explained for Everyone* (1997)

Peter Lynch, *One Up on Wall Street: How to Use What You Already Know To Make Money in the Market* (Simon & Schuster, 2000)

Matthew Lynn, *Bust: Greece, the Euro, and the Sovereign Debt Crisis* (Bloomberg UK, 2010)

B. Lietaer, C. Arnsperger, S. Brunnhuber and S. Goerner, *Money and Sustainability: The Missing Link* (Triarchy Press, 2012)

Charles Mackay, *Extraordinary Popular Delusions and the Madness of Crowds* (Wordsworth Reference, 1841, new edition 1995)

Burton Malkiel, *A Random Walk Down Wall Street: The Time-Tested Strategy for Successful Investing* (W.W. Norton & Co., 2012)

James O'Shaughnessy, *What Works on Wall Street: The Classic Guide to the Best-Performing Investment Strategies of All Time*, fourth edition (McGraw-Hill, 2011)

Carmen Reinhart and Kenneth Rogoff, *This Time Is Different: Eight Centuries of Financial Folly* (Princeton University Press, 2011)

Jack D. Schwager, *The New Market Wizards: Conversations with America's Top Traders* (HarperCollins, 1994)

Robert Shiller, *Irrational Exuberance*, second edition (Princeton University Press, 2005)

Jeremy Siegel, *Shares for the Long Run: The Definitive Guide to Financial Market Returns & Long-Term Investment Strategies* (McGraw-Hill, 2013)

Richard Tortoriello, *Quantitative Strategies for Achieving Alpha: The Standard and Poor's Approach to Testing Your Investment Choices* (McGraw-Hill Finance & Investing, 2008)